WELCOME TO THE STUPIDPOCALYPSE

WELCOME TO THE STUPIDPOCALYPSE

Survival Tips for the Dumbageddon

BRITTLESTAR
(STEWART REYNOLDS)

A POST HILL PRESS BOOK

ISBN: 979-8-88845-597-5
ISBN (eBook): 978-1-63758-840-6

Welcome to the Stupidpocalypse:
Survival Tips for the Dumbageddon

Cover design by Cody Corcoran
Cover photo by Terry Manzo

Post Hill Press, LLC
New York • Nashville
posthillpress.com

Published in the United States of America

For Shannon, who knows just how stupid I am.

CONTENTS

Politics Is Awful

Marriage Is Wonderful

America Is a Nice Idea

Secrets Canadians Keep

Family Are the Other People on the Plane Before It Crash Landed in the Jungle

Technology Is Obsolete

INTRODUCTION

Let's get one thing absolutely clear...we're all stupid and we all do dumb things.

I'm defining "stupid" here by its commonly referred use for the past hundred plus years or so as actions freed from the shackles of logic, reason, self-preservation, common sense, and evident success in the opposing action.

I'm defining "dumb" here as...those actions.

We all do things without thinking them through.

We all do things impulsively. Propelled by emotion.

Things like lashing out, quitting a job, saying no to dessert, getting married, buying that shirt that the young, cool sales clerk said suited you, or thinking that social media was a good idea.

We're all stupid and we all do dumb things.

And we've been that way forever.

Even since before the days Grog said to Oorg, "I bet I can sneak up on that sleeping mammoth."

I think you can imagine how that turned out for Grog without me going into much detail. Unless you believe it went well for Grog. Then maybe as a member of the Make Everything Grog Again (MEGA) group, this book might not be for you. But thanks for buying it!

So what is this Stupidpocalypse I refer to? Well, reader, here's the deal…

At some point in recent history, let's say…around when the USA decided it might be funny to let a two-dimensional cartoon of a businessman notorious for making bad decisions make decisions that would affect the whole planet, the Stupidpocalypse began.

You see, up until that point being stupid and doing dumb things was a cause for embarrassment. If you had been stupid and did something dumb, you did your best to conceal that fact or mitigate any damage.

However, suddenly it was okay to ignore evidence… replace facts with hunches…regard opinion as truth…and somehow not laugh when saying things like "alternative facts."

Don't like how something is going? Remember it differently!

Don't like this factual account of something? Make up your own!

Accountability became as passé as the word "slacks."

Many people learned that if you do enough stupid things in rapid succession, it might be okay.

At least for a while.

Now, I should also clarify that this book will not simply bash the "right."

No, just as stupid needs no passport, it also exists on every part of the political spectrum.

It's just that the dumb things the "right" have been doing recently are less "funny haha" and more "funny oh my god we're all going to die," so they stand out more.

But don't fret…stupid, like a viral pandemic, doesn't care who you voted for.

However, it's important that we're aware of the Stupidpocalypse.

Renowned science fiction writer Ray Bradbury famously wrote a short story about a time traveler who stepped on a butterfly in the prehistoric past and changed the outcome of a presidential election in 2055.

The Stupidpocalypse is like that…except instead of one guy accidentally stepping on a butterfly, it's a bunch of people with cans of bug spray.

We need to be vigilant. We need to be…smarter. We need to at least gird our loins or any other parts of us that are dangerously ungirded.

As funny as a stupid person doing a dumb thing is, it can have potential impacts on real life.

Especially when there are multiple stupid people doing multiple dumb things.

For example, a drunk man being attacked by a Canada goose and trying to fist fight with it—funny.

Large groups of drunk people going around provoking and punching Canada geese at random is a problem (even if they are dicks sometimes and easy to provoke by calling them a "raccoon with a pilot's license" or "American").

Again, we're all stupid and we all do dumb things.

Stupid is indeed everywhere in varying degrees.

Politics doesn't have a stranglehold on dumb things.

Parenting, marriage, family, America, social media, technology, Canada, America (I mention it twice because of American Exceptionalism).

So, what to do about this Stupidpocalypse?

The first step is…don't panic.

Panicking leads to stupid decisions and doing dumb things and we're already quite full of those, thank you very much.

The second step is…read this book.

It won't provide any protection but it will hopefully provide distraction as you patiently wait for the world to finish spiraling into abject idiocy.

FOREWORD

BY RYAN REYNOLDS

We're not related, and I will not be able to write the Foreword for your book.

—Ryan Reynolds

Parenting Is a Joke

ANIMALS ARE BETTER PARENTS

SURVIVAL TIP: IF WORRIED THAT YOU ARE FAILING AS A PARENT, REMEMBER THAT GIRAFFES LET THEIR BABIES DROP SIX FEET TO THE GROUND WHEN THEY'RE BORN IN ORDER TO SNAP THE UMBILICAL CORD AND SHOCK THEM INTO THE WORLD, AND THEY TURN OUT JUST FINE.

I remember it very well.

I remember both of them actually.

I was in the room for the birth of both of my sons. Despite that deeply scarring and terrifying experience, I love them to bits and I am immensely proud of both of them. They are me, but far, far better. They may not have as large a social media following as I do, but that's not a measure of success. Well, it *is* a literal measure of success in a very real way, so I may be entirely wrong about them being completely better than me, but I'm still very proud of both of them.

I also vividly remember cutting their umbilical cords. You ever had undercooked calamari? It was like cutting that.

Rubbery and probably quite chewy (I didn't chew it off; I used scissors). I apologize if that puts you off undercooked calamari, but that's life. Also you shouldn't be eating undercooked calamari. It's gross.

It was also a very primal experience...cutting my sons' umbilical cords, not eating calamari. Though it's close. Watching new life emerge onto the planet right in front of your eyes reminds you of how we're all just animals...except, for the most part, we wear pants.

I also remember about three weeks into our first son's life, a neighbor popped by "to see the baby." It's around the three week point of being a parent that the novelty of having this new accessory in your life starts to wear a bit thin. I'm not saying you don't love your baby any less, it's just that the weight of keeping another person alive becomes very evident. Plus, you haven't slept in about...three weeks. The baby's cries melt into white noise like after a really loud rock concert when your hearing is basically just low-definition crackling. You love your baby so much but also...what the hell is the problem please tell me and will that make you stop crying?

Anyway, this neighbor stood at the door and asked to see our new baby. I don't think I said any words to her. I turned and fetched our infant son in his car seat and plunked him down in front of her and gestured the words, "That is baby. See baby? Yay."

She bent down and looking adoringly at his adorable little face, said words that sent a shiver down my spine: "Enjoy this time. This is the easy part."

I stared at her blankly. I forced a smile but still did not speak despite words like "fuck," "right," and "off" spinning in my mind.

She was right, of course.

We soon discovered that a baby that stays in the same spot when you put it down is A LOT easier to care for than one who immediately transforms into a diapered ninja as soon as you loosen your grip.

As your kids grow, the challenges don't stop, they just change. Until one day you're facing the same challenges as they are, except you're still their parent.

But back to the distressing birth scenes.

Seeing my children being born was a privilege. As I said, it also felt a bit primal. You start to feel a way that can only be described as that thing that makes you retract your hand from a burning hot oven before you even know it's hot. It's spinal. It's visceral. It's animalistic.

Which makes you look at things differently. Suddenly you start crying at bathroom tissue commercials. You start to hate/love "Cat's in the Cradle" by Harry Chapin because it hits like a spike to your heart. You start to anthropomorphize animals and their relationship to their offspring.

But then you read up on animals and how they treat their offspring and realize they may actually be better parents than we humans are.

Every parent wants their child to grow up to be strong, independent, and resilient, yet none of us feel comfortable dropping an infant from six feet in the air when it's born like giraffes do.

Every parent cherishes the time they may get to spend breastfeeding their child...but not until they're eight years old like orangutans do. Freakin' weirdos.

Every parent wants to protect their child from the elements and harsh environment, yet not for months on end like emperor penguins do.

Every parent wants to provide for their child and leave them something, yet very few of us get to leave territory and food supplies like red squirrels do when they die.

Animals really do a great job at parenting. Though I would stop at saying we could learn a thing or two from them. At least not literally and directly.

Case in point, the Strawberry Poison Dart Frog father urinates on the eggs laid by his partner to keep them moist. I feel fairly confident that my wife, Shannon, wouldn't have been keen for me to try that when she was pregnant.

To be honest, I'm not sure I even could. (Bashful bladder.)

Therein lies my point: animals are better parents, kinda. The dad frog is like, "I've drank like six frog-sized beers, and I am ready to do my duty." I don't know if I could be that good of a parent. Maybe, I guess. If everyone did it. This is creating some distressing imagery in my head.

My point is…animal parents focus on what will keep their kids alive and thriving.

We could learn a thing or two from them. But again, and I cannot stress this enough, maybe not the peeing thing.

DIGITAL UMBILICAL CORD

SURVIVAL TIP: TRY TO MAINTAIN A HEALTHY AND SAFE LEVEL OF PLAUSIBLE DENIABILITY TOWARD YOUR CHILDREN.

I can say with 100 percent authority, that when I was a child, I was glad there were times my parents had no idea where I was or what I was doing.

From smoking horrendous menthol cigarettes (your entire existence can smell like an ashtray with a half-sucked mint in it!) behind the grocery store across the street from our home to being chased out of a then-illegal cannabis field by people with rifles on the back of a truck. We "accidentally" discovered the field by an abandoned farmhouse when we went there to climb up the side of the half-gone silo to see the dead pig floating in rainwater about thirty feet below. Good times, good times.

There exists a time in every child's development where the inner idiot must be indulged. Stupid must conquer reason occasionally.

Consequences must be made evidently real and give you a pretty good scare. And being chased by cannabis growers with rifles on the back of a pickup was a pretty good scare.

I feel this is essential for the healthy evolution from "little idiot" to "big stupid adult who should really know better." (I feel that I should note that in Canada, where I live, cannabis is legal and those folks with rifles on the back of a pickup are now probably legally selling their wares in a store called Mom's Favorite Cannabis.)

To be clear, I'm not one of the people who say, "When I was kid, our parents would send us out at the start of the day and not expect to see us again until the streetlights came on!"

No. I mean, it's largely true, but that's just lazy parenting.

As a human parent, you have a certain level of responsibility for the safeguarding of your spawn. These days, sending children out at the crack of dawn and having them unaccounted for for hours seems somewhat, if not absolutely, irresponsible.

That may have been the thing back in our day, but so was the unprescribed over-consumption of valium by some parents.

And sure, the kids who survived grew up to have some formidable life skills, but the same could be said about those people who finally get rescued after being lost for thirty days in the wilderness and look a little uncomfortable when asked about what they ate to survive, and by the way, what happened to their friend?

There has to be a balance for parents. Somewhere between "police state" and "betcha don't have the guts, fate."

Text messaging is in that sweet spot, I think. It can provide the illusion of immediate assurance of safety from child to parent and it can simultaneously provide global reach for one of a parent's most effective parenting tools...guilt.

Technology has brought us many benefits, but the notion that I can, from the comfort of my couch, fire a short, seemingly innocuous, and loving message to my children no matter where they are on the globe that I know will explode like an atomic guilt bomb and keep them in check is wonderful.

These messages are not directives or admonishments. There is no need for "Please be careful" or "Don't do anything dangerous." No, no...the secret is to disguise them as offers. Let me give you some examples of messages and their translation.

> Message: "Hope you're having fun!"
>
> Translation: "Don't come home late and make the loudest bowl of cereal ever."
>
> Message: "Just wanted to let you know I'm so proud of you!"
>
> Translation: "Put down the vape. You look like a futuristic idiot."
>
> Message: "Your teeth look so good since you got your braces off!"
>
> Translation: "I don't care how cool the dead pig is, get down from the ladder on that silo."

It's truly the perfect union between technology and parenting. An easy way to kink the digital umbilical cord and remind your children that you love them and they better appreciate that.

But of course, like all good things, you can go too far.

One of the coolest things you can do with mobile phones is find people's exact locations. For this reason, getting your child a mobile phone of their own so you can track their whereabouts seems like a good idea.

And it is…for a time.

If your child is younger, say "watches SpongeBob because it's funny" young, then yes, a good thing.

This technological wonder will allow you to confirm that they are indeed at the park.

This ensures that they are indeed where they are supposed to be.

If your child falls into the slightly older "watches SpongeBob because…dude, this show still rocks, dude…heh heh" category, you may not want to know where they are.

Hear me out…

Think back to the places you would be when you were in your teens.

Not the every-weekend-hangout spot of your friend's basement or garage, I mean the weird places that boredom or curiosity would take you to.

The places where you learned how to do that thing that you still do as your party trick today.

The places where you found out who you are…or more frequently, who you aren't.

Now imagine your parents knowing where you were during those times.

Questions would demand to be asked. Answers would satisfy no one and the whole experience would make you determined to outwit being tracked.

That's not good for anyone.

We're lucky to live in this age where we can check in with our kids no matter where we or they are.

We just have to make sure we don't abuse it.

HOW TO CHOOSE YOUR FAVORITE CHILD

SURVIVAL TIP: CHOOSING A FAVORITE CHILD IS LIKE CHOOSING A FAVORITE CAR TIRE. ONCE IN MOTION, YOU'RE STUCK WITH THE ONES YOU'VE GOT AND YOU WANT THEM ALL TO PERFORM WELL.

I was once asked who was my favorite child.

I replied that the kid next door, Kelsey, seemed pretty good as far as kids go.

Then I realized they were specifically referring to my two sons.

Should you have children, you may already know this, and if you don't, it's about time you did.

If you don't have children and someday hope to, it's important you know this as well.

There is no benefit to choosing a favorite child. Despite how maddeningly frustrating one or more may be at any given time, your favorite one will turn on you eventually.

Children, I was shocked to initially discover, are not carbon copies of their parents. Sure, they may look like you, act like you, think like you to an extent—and actually, that's pretty annoying sometimes too, now that I think about it.

Children are their own beings. They are merely other humans you have created and/or guided into life. And we can all agree that humans are awful and by that reasoning, your children are awful too. This realization, while initially harsh, will provide you comfort as we discuss this issue further.

Choosing a favorite child is foolhardy. It is the equivalent of choosing a favorite tire on your car...while doing 80 mph on the highway. You may begrudge how much they cost, how they're impossible to keep clean, how they seem to be making too much noise...but you ultimately want and need all of them to perform well.

What happens if some time in the future you're old, frail, and in need of help and your favorite child is unable to come provide assistance and you're stuck with the other children who know they aren't the favorite? I'll tell you what happens... what happens is you better not have any problems with your email because your also-rans offspring aren't going to help.

No, there is no benefit to choosing a favorite child.

What you need to do is stay flexible. Instead of choosing a favorite, recognize there will be times that one or more of your children may be entirely unlikeable. Again, they're just humans. Humans that you have to buy food and expensive sneakers for.

Stay flexible and choose your least favorite(s). Acknowledge this will change. Make them work for your love.

I realize this may sound cruel and could promote rivalry between siblings.

Well, only if you're lucky.

Imagine waking up on the weekend and your children are racing to be the first to cut the lawn, clean the kitchen, or vacuum the living room. All vying for your approval and the coveted status of "favorite child." All the while you know that it doesn't exist.

Finally, you can get back at your children for not knowing if they mean good or bad when they say something is "dead-ass." For that time they freaked out at Applebee's even though they knew it was the closest you'd come to a fancy meal out since they were born.

Yes, there is benefit to letting your children know that the title of "Favorite Child" is constantly up for grabs.

However, it must be noted that you may never publicly state or even decide who has that title. You can only let them know they do *not* have it currently *but* they could if things go well.

To be clear, I am no parenting expert or licensed family psychologist, so this advice is purely anecdotal and largely fabricated. If you've purchased this book because you thought I looked like a parenting expert or licensed family psychologist, you're right, but that's on you.

If, upon seeing my own two grown children in their early twenties, you think I've done a good job parenting because my kids turned out alright so I must be a reliable source for excellent parenting tips, you're right. Though that would be like asking a lottery winner for tips on how to win the lottery.

Declaring a favorite child is stupid. Each child is a blessing/windfall. Treat them as such.

Each and every child will ebb and flow, make mistakes, learn, make more mistakes, learn more, make you proud, drive you insane, bring you peace…just like every human ever.

They all deserve a chance to be the Favorite Child…even though they already are.

SARCASTIC TRUTH IS ALWAYS THE BEST OPTION

SURVIVAL TIP: TRUTH IS ALWAYS THE BEST OPTION, ESPECIALLY WHEN ADMITTED WITH A SARCASTIC TONE.

They had gone away for a week.

A work convention in Arizona. My dad took Mom and they decided to do what everyone does at work conventions, which is work as little as possible and enjoy it as a vacation.

I was fifteen years old and my sister was seven. It was decided that my sister would stay with my grandparents for the week. Their home was only a few short blocks away. I somehow (miraculously, really) convinced my parents that I was mature enough to stay on my own at home. I made the argument that I would check-in with my grandparents every day by phone and in the event of an emergency, my grandparents could be on scene quick smart. By "quick smart" I mean within about a fifteen minute walk or a thirty minute bus ride with transfer at the depot because neither of them drove a car.

My parents were good parents to me growing up. Still are. They tolerated many tantrums, freak-outs, blow-outs, big plans, big plans gone awry, and the usual list of childhood and adolescent unpleasantness.

However, in hindsight as a parent now, I feel this decision to leave me unattended at home…for a week…with a car in the driveway…in a week that included a Halloween weekend…was one of their poorer parenting moments.

That said, it was a great week.

Like, it was a *really* great week.

After many briefings on dos and don'ts, which were cherubically and pensively agreed to, my parents headed to the airport.

I immediately picked up the phone and called my two friends and told them the coast was clear for a week-long sleepover.

We began innocently enough: deciding upon a mutually favored supper time of 6:30 p.m. Growing up, my parents never had dinner at the dining table together. We ate dinner anywhere in the house. Watching TV, listening to music in my room, downstairs playing video games. The dining table was only used when we had houseguests and for the holidays when my dad crafted a folding table that was deployed in the living room and was so big that no one had to leave their spot on the chairs or sofa. Genius.

So, establishing this civilized supper hour where myself and my two friends would convene at the dining table and eat together already felt rebellious.

The surface tension of propriety as defined in our family household had been broken. Other rules crumbled quickly.

Spending most of our days together at school and after meant that the conversation between us friends quickly stagnated. It was decided that we would pull up a fourth chair and invite the family dog, Benji, to eat his dinner at the same time and on the same table. Benji, probably feeling the same thrill of bucking convention as the rest of us did, politely sat up on the chair and ate from his bowl. Though beyond his jovial furry presence, he brought little to the conversation.

As Halloween night approached, it was decided that we would hand out candy to the neighborhood kids, and then at around 8 p.m., we would head to a local bar that was having a Halloween party. I remind you, I was fifteen. However, my two friends were sixteen, which meant our combined age was forty-seven and there are many forty-seven-year-olds at bars. We got our costumes on and headed out the door. The bar was decorated in its spooky best and spirits were high, some most likely stoned. Now, before you get concerned about a bar allowing underage teens to drink, they didn't. We drank vanilla Cokes all night. They made us take the bottle of wine we won as a door prize home.

We were now accelerating toward the don'ts I had been briefed on. But hey, the dog at the dinner table had gone so well, why not?

Girlfriends were invited back. The Mateus was opened and shared. Teenage hormones ran rampant. The dog, fearing losing his newly acquired seat at the table, looked the other way.

The day after was a Professional Activities (PA) Day. No school. The girls left early. The rest of us decided we would seek the answer to the age old question, "Can you fry escargots in butter and Hai Karate cologne?"

The answer is yes. More specifically, yes with lots of blue flames and bad-tasting escargot.

The debauchery raged on.

"Hey, can I borrow the car?" my sixteen-year-old unlicensed friend asked with an expression on his face that suggested this was a completely reasonable request.

I paused to consider the potential consequences of saying yes.

However, as I was fifteen, I could not foresee any. Though I did feel we needed to take precautions. Not for the very real dangers of the operation of an automobile in a real world setting, but rather so that I wouldn't get caught for moving the car when my parents got home. Which was one of the items on the quickly diminishing don'ts list that we hadn't do-ed yet.

A plan was hatched. We would chalk mark where the wheels were in the driveway. Anyone using the car would then return it to the exact spot. The car was a tiny hatchback, so failing the exact positioning, we would simply lift to adjust. Seriously. And we did.

We would also note the gas gauge and make sure there was an identical amount of gas in the tank before my parents returned. *Ferris Bueller's Day Off* hadn't been released yet, so we didn't even think about the odometer.

Various journeys were enjoyed and enjoyed safely. We marveled at the convenience of just being able to go anywhere in town. We radiated machismo at being able to pick up and drop off our girlfriends at their whim. We thrilled at going ten clicks above the city speed limit on the edge of town (still within the speed limit but it felt way faster).

Then it happened.

A minor thing, but still, it complicated things.

I was reversing out of our driveway and, because I was an untrained, unlicensed, and moronic fifteen-year-old, I backed into our metal fence pole. I felt the metal of the fence pole yield to the soft metal of the back passenger side fender. I got out to survey the damage and noted the considerable dent in the fender, the scratched paint, and the slightly bent fence pole.

Another plan was hatched. Teenagers spend a lot of time hatching plans.

We would use tools to bang out the dent.

We would use model paint from a nearby corner store to touch up the scratched paint.

It was a ridiculous attempt at hiding what had happened.

Thankfully, it was a ridiculous attempt that worked.

My friends returned to their homes. My parents arrived back from the convention.

They scanned the house and noticed nothing out of the ordinary, apart from the dog's bowl on the dining table. Which prompted them to ask how things went when they were away.

It was at that moment that I learned a valuable lesson.

Panicked that I would spin a web that would be contradicted by my friends or myself later, I decided to go with the truth. But I would admit all with a sarcastic tone.

"My friends stayed all week, the dog ate dinner at the table with us every night, we went to a bar, won a bottle of wine, brought some girls back to the house, fried up some snails in cologne, and used the car all week."

The room went quiet.

"You did not!" my mother exclaimed.

"Yeah, we *totally* did," I replied in the most sarcastic voice I could muster.

My parents laughed and it was over.

Lying is never good. It's tiring and requires more effort than it's worth.

The truth is always the best option…provided you can tell it in a sarcastic tone.

Also, if you can throw in a weird detail like a dog with good table manners, you're golden.

My parents still don't know the whole story.… Well, I guess they do now.

YOU ARE NOT YOUR CHILDREN

SURVIVAL TIP: YOUR CHILDREN MAY BE MADE UP OF PART OF YOU BY NATURE OR NURTURE BUT THEY WILL STILL BE THEIR OWN PEOPLE DESPITE HOW ANNOYING AND/OR TERRIFYING THAT IS TO YOU.

It certainly seemed weird to me.

It was certainly not something I would have done.

Thoughts raced through my head about how weird it seemed.

My father-in-law had been sitting upright on the couch at the cottage with our six-month-old son in his lap. Then, he decided he'd have a bit of a lie down, and that seemed to coincide with our son's sleepy expression. So my father-in-law placed him on his chest and the two of them napped. Together.

First thought in my new parent brain: "Yikes, I wouldn't do that." Like there is a world where the option of having a nap all snuggled in and cozied up on my father-in-law's chest would be there for me to take. That description makes it sound like I might want to. I do not want to.

It was the first time I had properly disconnected, in a healthy way, from our son. He was no longer an accessory to my life and was his own person. His own person who sleeps on my father-in-law's chest, right there in the living room, and he seems to be snuggling in and...GAHHHHH! WHAT THE HELL?! No...no...he's a baby and he's sleeping on his grandfather's chest. Very different. It is, right? Sure, it is. Totally normal. Completely normal.

As parents, we feel so connected to our kids. We try really hard to see the world through their eyes. We strain to be as empathetic as possible so we can understand them and how they feel about the things they encounter. I think that's important, but I also think it's potentially a slippery slope from empathy to thinking of them as a little you that gets to start again.

If you have kids, you probably know exactly what I mean.

If you don't have kids, you are probably starting to understand that everyone's parents are crazy.

But it's not entirely the fault of us parents. Kids are just so damn sponge-like when it comes to interests. If we love music, we probably play music in the house when they're growing up and they end up loving music. That's a good thing. That's a nice thing. There's usually even a nice crossover portion of their young lives where the music they like is the music we like. But then comes the day when they share their preferred music with you and it makes no sense. It's too loud, it's too crass, or worse...it's country.

It's not just interests, of course. It's also skills, both physical and mental. If you're athletic and like to play tennis, your kid probably grows up around a lot of tennis and invariably wants to play tennis as well. Likewise, if you were good at school (that string of words lets you know how 'good at school' I was), your kid is probably going to be a pretty good academic as well.

But here's the thing...just because your kid may share interests or skills with you does not mean they exist as a do-over for the things you should have or should not have done. They may jive along to your playlist one day and then tell you the next that one of your favorite Scritti Politti songs sounds like Super Mario background music. They may love playing tennis with you for ages and then suddenly decide disc golf is a far better sport. They may have shared your keen mathematical mind when they were younger, but now they do better in drama class.

Your children are not you.

And that's okay.

In fact, it's great.

Though your children are their own people, they remain permanently connected to you. Whether they like it or not. By nature or nurture, they are little versions of you. They're still not *you*, but they are versions of you. This means that, although you may not be able to coerce them to chase the dreams you weren't able to catch when you were their age, it does mean that they may get to do a myriad of things you would never have thought of or had the courage to do.

You are not your children.

But if you're lucky...your children are you, but better.

Social Media Is the Big Bad World

THE FREE SPEECH MYTH

SURVIVAL TIP: IF SOMEONE COMPLAINS THAT THEIR FREE SPEECH IS UNDER THREAT AND THEY DON'T CURRENTLY LIVE IN A COMMUNIST (OR OTHER) DICTATORSHIP, THEY ARE REFERRING TO THEIR RIGHT TO SAY WHATEVER THEY WANT DESPITE HOW WRONG, HURTFUL, DAMAGING, RACIST, A LOT OF OTHER *ISTS, AND PLAIN STUPID IT MAY BE.

We don't have "freedom of speech" in Canada.

We have "freedom of expression," which is largely the same idea, but for a moment there I had some pseudo-trucker convoy types apoplectic with the idea that I had just given the game away.

The First Amendment to the United States Constitution allows US citizens the freedom to express themselves without censorship, interference, and restraint by the government.

Here in Canada, our Freedom of Expression is regarded as a fundamental freedom...within reason. Meaning we're not so cool with hate speech, obscenity, and defamation going willy-nilly.

Both Canada and the US recognize freedom of expression and free speech as essential to a civilized and free society. However, neither of them regard it as *carte blanche* to be an absolute dickhead.

The notion that free speech can be a free for all and still be Utopian is a myth.

People are awful.

There is a reason that the expression, "Give someone an inch and they'll take a mile" was coined. In fact, it was lifted from a book from 1546 by John Heywood, where it was originally "Give him an inch and he'll take an ell." An "ell" being a unit of measurement of around forty-five inches.

If Mr. Heywood were around today, he could be forgiven for seeing his bastardized phrase and saying, "See?"

Yes, people are awful and generally stupid. They will often mistake freedom as license to be their worst. They will treat a buffet as their own personal food trough, paying little heed to any other diners and making us all praise the inventor of the Sneeze Guard. They will take a penny from those trays at corner stores and never leave one. They will treat those little mini libraries put up in front yards for the community as their own personal free bookstore.

People are awful.

This is why I cringe at the cries of those in any democratic country who say their free speech is being infringed upon. It's not. They just don't like the rules, and they want to say awful things.

When Elon Musk purchased Twitter, he promised to bring back free speech to the app, and instances of the N-word on the platform apparently skyrocketed by 500 percent.

That's not free speech. That's just people who want to say terrible things.

Humans require ground rules. We require parameters. Freedom without parameters in place to protect the marginalized is not freedom, it is mob rule at best and rule by intimidation or force at worst.

Free speech requires rules so that we can all be...well... free to speak without fear. But that requires some rules in place to make sure our free speech doesn't infringe upon someone else's.

Freedom without parameters is mayhem.

Free speech without parameters is chaos.

Those that may argue "sticks and stones may break my bones, but words will never hurt me," and doubt the real-world power of words, have apparently never seen a Happy Hour sign or read a STOP sign.

Words have power. They can do immeasurable damage and undeniable good. However, like any power, they need to be grounded to the best interests of society. The idea that we could all just say what we want all the time anytime and things would somehow be better in the world is laughable. My right to speak freely cannot override your right and vice versa.

Though we still have some people who believe that having freedom to say whatever you want would be like living in Utopia. And they're correct, but only in that Utopia, an ancient Greek word, literally translates to "No Place."

Social media tries hard every now and then to be that "No Place." It attempts to offer the free-for-all freedom of speech that some people think would be good...and it never works out.

Back in 2013, an app called Yik Yak allowed users to anonymously post on a feed that was exclusive to a geographic radius of five miles. Within days of it being downloaded, it was the app of choice for cyberbullying, which resulted in it being banned from numerous schools and then eventually closing its doors in 2017. The app has since relaunched in 2021 and is claiming to be much more moderated. Proving, to me at least, that the only thing worse than people who think they're allowed to say anything is anonymous people who think they're allowed to say anything.

Humans have proven time and time again that they can't handle fully free speech. We spiral into shouty masses of idiots all desperate to be heard but not held accountable for our words.

Thankfully, we don't really have 100 percent free speech and that's good.

BE EVERYWHERE YOUR KIDS DON'T WANT YOU TO BE

SURVIVAL TIP: FLEX YOUR PARENTAL POWERS OF "PARENTING BY THREAT OF EMBARRASSMENT" BY LEARNING THE LATEST TIKTOK DANCE.

It was about 8:40 p.m. when the friend request came in on my computer screen.

Nothing too unusual about that, but then I double-took at the name: Gregor Reynolds.

Our youngest son, Gregor, had been hired to play the role of Astyanax in a professional production of *The Trojan Women*. It's a dark Greek tragedy and Gregor's character was thrown to his death every night from a tower. He loved it.

Gregor was five years old when he was hired but was now the ripe old age of six and apparently fleshing out his Facebook account with some new friends.

As you can imagine, we were horrified.

Mainly because we knew he went on stage each performance at 8:45 p.m. and as his parents we felt responsible for making sure he arrived on stage on cue, but then we remembered they have people for that...but also because he was six years old and sending out friend requests on social media.

I accepted his friend request and messaged him right away.

"Don't you have to be on stage in a few minutes?"

"Yep!" came the reply. Then radio silence.

This all happened well before I was a professional social media darling. Social media was still just a distraction for me and many. Not an all-consuming beast that must be fed with 24/7 scrolling, likes, and misinformed acidic hot takes.

Shannon and I discussed what to do. We wanted to be good parents and wanted to be realistic about the fact that Gregor would likely just go online again when he could. His older brother, Owen, was already online at nine years old.

We decided that he could keep his Facebook account but wasn't allowed to post where he lived, what school he went to, or a profile picture of himself. The profile picture restriction seemed reasonable, if a little futile, though as he had just been named and pictured in a full above-the-fold article in a national newspaper about the production he was in.

Gregor didn't mind though. He said he was happy to draw his own profile picture and he did. A stick man, slightly bent at the waist with a green fart cloud exiting his backend.

We were so proud.

As part of our decision to allow our entirely too young children on the big bad world of social media, we decided we would make a concerted effort to be wherever they were. We would keep a close eye on them by being omnipresent. A bit like taking your kid to the park but always being in sight and shouting distance. It lets them gain some independence but you're also at the ready if things go pear-shaped on the jungle gym.

As the boys grew into adolescence, of course, it became harder to police them all the time. However, that didn't change our plan. It felt more important than ever to be where they were. We couldn't swaddle them in bubble-wrap (I feel that may be an asphyxiation risk anyway), but we could at least have a little bit of an idea of the parks they were playing in.

"Sure," I hear you thinking to yourself (or maybe out loud, I don't know what kind of weirdo you are), "but you make a living being an idiot on social media. It's easy for you and your hair is amazing."

That's all true, but it turns out you don't have to be a professional and stunningly good-looking moron like me in order to set up a social media account.

If your kids are on YouTube...get on YouTube.

If your kids are on TikTok...get on TikTok.

If your kids are on LinkedIn...they're old enough to take care of themselves, so maybe back off, MOM.

You may not be able to protect them from every horrible thing, but at least you'll have a better idea of what the hell they're talking about when they say they're planning a duet with someone using that TikTok sound that guy made that's trending.

Which will hopefully make it easier for you to provide guidance and advice.

Which is all you really can do once your kids reach a certain age.

Well...that and learn how to do TikTok dances so you can still threaten them.

EVERY IDIOT HAS A MEGAPHONE

SURVIVAL TIP: ALWAYS REMEMBER THAT EVERYONE IS ENTITLED TO AN OPINION AND THANKS TO SOCIAL MEDIA WE GET TO HEAR ALL OF THEM WHETHER WE LIKE IT OR NOT. LEARN TO IGNORE THE DUMB ONES.

I've been online since about 1992.

Not continuously. I had to hang up every now and then so I could use the phone.

I've been online continuously, in one way or another, since probably 2001.

I've been in awe of the internet since I first patiently waited for the crackles, beeps, whirrs, and squeals of my modem to connect me to CompuServe or AOL in the early '90s. It was the very dawn of the graphic world wide web we know today and it was exciting. It couldn't have happened at a better time for me. I was on my own a lot in a new city and I felt a little isolated...but the internet changed that.

I could be part of Usenet groups that discussed a multitude of topics. I could connect with a young woman in California who was also a David Sylvian fan and get her to check the local record shop for any rare new releases for me. Unthinkable only a few years earlier.

It was truly magical and I loved spending time online. Despite having to pay 10¢ per minute for the long-distance dial-up number, it really made me feel like I was part of the world.

Fast-forward to the mid-2000s and the advent of social media. We went from sharing relevant information about specific topics with like-minded people to just…shouting in to the void? Bellowing in the digital market square?

Suddenly, thanks to social media, every idiot had a megaphone.

I need to clarify here that when I say "idiot," I mean all of us. Every single one.

Yes, even you. Definitely me.

This was tremendously empowering at first. A way for those voices that hadn't been heard to finally be heard. That's a wonderful thing and there are many wonderful things people can say via social media that are VERY worth listening to. There are conversations that need to happen. There are messages that must be relayed. There are perspectives that are vital to the survival of one or many.

That's all very important stuff and we should make an attempt to focus on that stuff.

But it's difficult.

Again, every idiot has a megaphone.

So, in amongst the messages that deserve to be heard are the nonsensical (if you're lucky), racist, homophobic, misogynistic, transphobic, and every other kind of dickhead, rantings of the truly most idiotic.

And somehow they seem to have louder megaphones.

So, what's to do?

Well, as someone who spends an inordinate amount of time on social media and creates content for social media, I like to think of it as a busy pub or bar.

Busy pubs are great. The atmosphere is usually electric with many voices all sharing stories, jokes, and confessions. However, regardless of what pub you're in, you can almost guarantee that as the night wears on, there will be a growing number of morons. The ones who, upon hearing the many other voices in the room, feel compelled to get attention for themselves at any cost.

If these people are sitting at your table, you leave the table.

If these people are standing beside you at the bar, you find a different spot.

If these people are yelling out ridiculous comments or takes as you pass them on the way back from the bathroom, you most likely do not stop and ask them to elaborate in a lengthy back and forth discussion.

In all of these scenarios, the trick is to ignore the stupidity and move on to enjoy your time.

The same rules apply to social media. Social media is a wonderful thing that has empowered many voices that need to be heard, plus some voices that are just fun to hear. However, it has also given some of us the false sense that all opinions are equal and deserve to be heard.

They do not.

They absolutely do not.

The mere thought that they do ignores all other factors of the person delivering their opinion. It ignores where the opinion came from and why it came.

While when the greasy drunk man who yells at you as you pass in the pub that oooh, he'd "do good things to that choo-choo" may be his opinion, it does not mean it is valid or merits listening to. No offence to your "choo-choo"...whatever he meant by that. I'm guessing he meant "caboose" but was unable to find that word.

Social media presents all voices as equal (to an extent), but of course they are not. Just like that crowded noisy pub.

Some voices are worth listening to and some are best ignored.

EVERY POST IS AN ENDORSEMENT

SURVIVAL TIP: WITHOUT ADDITIONAL COMMENTARY, EVERYTHING YOU SHARE ON SOCIAL MEDIA WILL BE SEEN AS YOUR ABSOLUTE MANIFESTO.

"Shared posts are not endorsements."

Uh, yes they are.

I follow you and you shared the post. You chose to amplify it. You thought to yourself, "Hey, I want everyone who follows me to see this."

And we did. And we can only assume it was because you felt the same way or shared the same view or wholeheartedly agreed with the original post and poster.

Of course, that isn't necessarily true. However, in the absence of any commentary from you, we only see those words you've amplified as your own.

Such is the beauty and the curse of social media. Every person has a voice and when we follow you, we assume it's your voice. We even read things in your voice. Don't believe me? Read anything Patton Oswalt shares and try to not hear the words in his deceptively mellifluous and earnest tones.

I've always found it funny when otherwise incredibly intelligent people on social media put these "shared posts are not endorsements" type caveats in their bios...like anyone is reading their bios or at the very least has even bothered reading since clicking the follow button. Like we'd see a shared post of an incendiary article with an indefensible stance on an important issue and immediately go to their bio to see if this shared post was indeed an endorsement or not.

Nonsense. The immediate assumption is that it is an endorsement.

The beauty of social media is the addictive and weird parasocial relationships it offers. We cradle the world in our hands while we're on the toilet. We stare into the eyes of someone on a video when we're otherwise alone on the subway. It's an intimate relationship that is based on assumed, even if cavalierly assumed, trust. That's what makes it great and makes it feel authentic and genuine.

It feels like we're hearing directly from you. And, unless you're somebody who has someone ghost-writing their social posts, we are. That's pretty great.

It provides a thrill when we connect with people online because we assume that their fingers typed out the message. When I first tweeted Henry Winkler with a picture of me wearing my favorite The Fonz t-shirt when I was eight and he *replied*...I lost my mind. THE FONZ HAS A PHONE AND HE SPENT TIME ON IT TO COMMUNICATE WITH ME.

That's the real intangible value of social media. It still really feels person-to-person.

So, if I present an article to you, the assumption is that I agree with the article; I'm sending it to you and that means I want to share this thing I agree with, with you.

Kind of like if I just silently passed you a copy of *Mein Kampf* and offered no reason or explanation. You'd be like, "this guy must think this is a good book...what a weirdo... hasn't he seen *Raiders of the Lost Ark*?"

Or if I passed you some anti-vax literature and didn't say anything. Just handed you a bunch of dumbass brochures and walked away. It would be fair for you to assume that I was not very bright in general and a science-averse goon specifically.

Everything you post on social media is an endorsement... for or against. The closest you can come to middle ground is to comment, "I'm not too sure about this," and even then, we think you're just too scared to admit you agree and you're feeling things out before you jump in with both feet.

This is why it seems very important to be aware of whose posts you're amplifying on social media. I think we can all think of a time when we've come across a post that is so ridiculous we felt compelled to share it so others can see how ridiculous it is. But without bluntly stating, "Hey, look at how ridiculous this is," people will have no way to know that you, in fact, think it's ridiculous.

Again, I think it all ties back to the intimate relationships we feel we have with those we follow on social media. If you and I met on the street, and I said directly to you with no context, "Nice to meet you in person! Hey, seriously...I think the election was stolen by the Shriners. I've seen videos and they can fit two, maybe up to three ballot boxes in each of those tiny cars...and they have thousands of those tiny cars," you'd have to assume I at least kinda believed what I was saying to you.

In fact, unless I then followed up with "Can you believe those morons believe that?" you would assume that I was one of the morons.

Inferential Social Media hasn't been invented yet. Every post is an endorsement.

MEN AND SOCIAL MEDIA: WORLD WIDE WEB OF WIENERS

SURVIVAL TIP: VERY FEW PEOPLE WANT TO SEE A PICTURE OF YOUR WIENER.

As we passed the table of four young men, one of them meowed.

Yes, meowed. Like a cat.

I'm not sure where you are, but I feel I can confidently assume that meowing at someone is an unusual act pretty much anywhere. But then again, if there are men where you are, it's entirely possible that it's not that unusual at all. Men are weird.

It's okay, as a man, I can say that.

Back to the meow...

I was with my girlfriend at the time and her workmate, another young woman, and we had arrived at a local bar to get a drink and a bite to eat. I was just about to describe my girlfriend and the other woman as attractive, but they were young and in their early twenties and that is usually enough to clear the bar of "attractive enough to illicit unwanted attention" for women. In fact, before I even finished writing that sentence, I thought some more and realized that women of any age clear the bar of "attractive enough to illicit unwanted attention" from men.

Again, we passed by their table and one of the young men meowed at the women. My girlfriend ignored it. I was taken aback and chortled (guys who meow at women, oddly, hate chortling.... I mean, if we're just making noises, why can't I choose a chortle?). The other woman responded with a polite "fuck off." Which just seemed to stir their pot, though it eventually settled and nothing else happened.

I'm not now, nor was I then, sure of what the success rate is for guys who meow at women.

Is there a variable ratio that warrants them to keep on doing it? Did one guy meow at a woman one time in history and she immediately turned on her high heel, pulled him close, and right before kissing him, said in a sexy voice, "Oh baby, that was the best Maine Coon impression I've ever heard. You're getting a can of wet food tonight"? And then that story has passed down through the ages and that guy in the bar we were at had heard tell of this success when he was growing up and thought "Why not?"

Maybe.

Cat people are weird.

It's okay, as a normal person, I can say that.

Now, all this to say, this is why men are horrible on social media.

As someone who spends an unhealthy amount of time on social media and has for decades now, I've seen men successfully take their awful behavior and transition it to the...online world (I had to go get my blue light blocking reading glasses to finish that sentence).

Men have been "shooting their shots" with women since the dawn of time. Social media has merely made that easier, and heaven help us all, anonymous.

Which makes their behavior all the more bizarre. It's like if that guy who meowed at my girlfriend and her friend saw us coming, hid somewhere in the bar, and then meowed as we came in.

"Did you hear a cat?" the women would ask.

"Teeheehee!"—the guy, crouched down behind a table, probably.

It's pointless.

Now, let me address the "not all men" crowd.... You're correct. Some of us dudes are trying to be sentient and capable of perceiving the world beyond our own Y-fronts and we're not all horrible. However, there are enough of us acting awful, so though it may be an overgeneralization, it feels fair. At least to varying degrees.

That some men have the notion that it's okay to message women online with romantic overtures (and I'm REALLY stretching the definition of "romantic overtures" here) based solely on their interaction with them via their phone or computer screen is laughable...if it weren't so goddamn creepy.

A good friend, actor, and online personality in the UK, Jayne Sharp (@JayneSharp) told me recently that "There isn't a day that goes by that some random bloke doesn't subject me to the pervy thoughts in his mind."

Who are these geniuses? What is their desired outcome? If not nefarious, do they think this will work? Do they think Jayne will one day throw caution, safety, and good sense to the wind and…and…fall in love with them? Or at least acquiesce and flirt back?

Actually, it's not "flirting" is it? Flirting can be innocent and fun. A compliment here and there but nothing over the line that may make the other person uncomfortable. Flirting is usually done in person, face to face, where you can make use of other cues and body language. Flirting also, and I'm guessing here, usually doesn't involve whipping out your wiener, waggling it about, and saying, "Hey, look at my wiener."

As Jayne went on to say, "I'd say the penis photos are less common, but still far more frequent than I'd prefer."

Which is hilarious, but again, also awful.

Another friend and successful entrepreneur, Amber Mac (@AmberMac) shared with me that because she works in the world of tech and business, she often gets men wanting to argue with her about politics and technology.… But she also said, "I will get dating inquiries from my newsletter subscribers and LinkedIn connections."

"Inquiries" is a nice, innocent word. I may be wrong, but it feels like Amber is describing her experiences graciously.

There may be a handful of times in history where it did, but I honestly have a hard time believing being a creep has ever worked out. Why do some men continue with this abhorrent behavior?

Has anyone ever attended a wedding where the groom stood to make his speech and said, "This fairy tale all started when I sent her a random message online. I had never spoken to her before, but I repeatedly asked her to send me her used underpants and then I sent a picture of my semi-flaccid gear shift and here we are!"

Social media has just allowed men to act stupid and do dumb things on a global scale. That dude who meowed probably got his first social media account and thought, "Now I can meow at random women all over the world from anywhere in the world! Social media is great!"

PREMATURE E-SPECULATION

SURVIVAL TIP: DON'T COMMENT ON A SOCIAL MEDIA POST OF AN ARTICLE OR PIECE OF MEDIA BASED SOLELY ON THE HEADLINE OR CAPTION. IT'S LIKE BUYING A PIE WITHOUT KNOWING WHAT KIND OF PIE IT IS.

Lots of men suffer from it.

Usually temporary, though sometimes chronic, the condition is normally caused by pre-existing bias, mounting online crapulence, or a general sense of "probably."

The condition is not exclusive to men, of course. Women can suffer as well.

It's also not exclusive to any one demographic, geographical region, or even political leaning.

No, it can affect any of us at any time.

It's called...Premature E-Speculation.

It's an embarrassing condition whereby the afflicted is seen by some to be a careless and reckless retweeter or commenter.

The condition causes social media users to prematurely speculate on the content of an article or piece of media based purely on the headline or caption.

In other words, the "speculation" on the part of the social media user is "premature."

The "e" part in "e-speculation" is for "electronic," but it's mainly just there to make sure the "premature ejaculation" joke lands. Thank you, thank you. I'll be here all week…or until you finish this book.

We've all fallen victim to Premature E-Speculation at some point, and if we haven't, we know someone who has and we're lying about the first part. There is just too much stuff on social media to actually properly read every single article and watch every single video. Opinions must be made, and they must be made fast.

In the endless scroll world of social media, it's entirely possible that whatever post you're reading at any given time will be less fabulous or less entertaining or more enraging than the next one, so any itch to react must be scratched quickly so you can get on to the next post. There is no time to discern if a headline or caption is factual or misleading. That requires investigation, time, comprehension, and acceptance of nuance.

Social media is no place for nuance. Much like real life, it is a stupid place full of people all trying to convince you to buy something or get you on their side. Yes, it's just like real life except faster, more convenient, and with less walking and you use your thumbs way more.

However, what we absolutely know is that Premature E-Speculation does not satisfy anyone.

It's all over too quickly.

Seeing a post that links to an article that supports your world view is quite thrilling. It's easy to hit the Share button. This is why Twitter implemented a prompt that asks if you'd like to read the article first before sharing it.

That's how bad of a problem Premature E-Speculation has become. Twitter, whose entire business plan is based on hot takes, half-truths, and handsome hunks (me), has decided that we're pulling the trigger a little too quickly. It has automated the position of sober second thought. It's like an AI version of your spouse looking over your shoulder and saying "Ya sure?"

So, what can be done to prevent this condition?

Well, it might be suggested that we train people to be smarter on social media.

To read articles in full and only then state their opinions.

To watch videos before assuming their content.

To listen first, then speak.

But, of course, that's not what makes social media fun... and why should the burden of comprehension be on the user?

Why should I, an average idiot, be required to change my idiot behavior? (This sentence, by the way, is one of the core reasons for the Stupidpocalypse.)

Let's instead remind all who post articles and videos on social media that the bare minimum amount of context—and I'm talking microscopic—will be digested prior to people commenting with great emotion.

Initially this sounds horrible, but hear me out.

In today's fast-paced endless scroll world, we need people to cut to the chase. I'm not saying abandon all long form content like books, newspaper articles, and videos over twenty seconds. No, those will still have their place and purpose...

like when you're guilted into consuming them by a loved one. This book being the exception, of course (though you will note that I have with great effort divided this book into bite-sized essays...I'm thoughtful that way).

What I'm saying is, we don't need to know the details if the headlines and captions are crystal clear.

For example...

THE QUEEN IS DEAD. SHE WAS OLD.

Got it. Queen of England was really old and now she's dead.

Or...

POLICE K-9 UNIT FIRED FOR RACE.

Crystal clear. Another casualty of the woke mob.

You see? It's easy.

Wait... I've just been told that it was actually the police dog handlers who were fired because they were racing the dogs against each other.

...

...

...

I guess I should've read the full story before commenting.

THE NEW MAINSTREAM MEDIA

SURVIVAL TIP: REMIND YOURSELF THAT WHEN COMPLAINING ABOUT THE MEDIA ON SOCIAL MEDIA, YOU ARE THE MEDIA ON SOCIAL MEDIA.

In the bigger picture, it wasn't that consequential.

I completely understood the grief and shock, but no one had died.

The large rock formation had stood on the shoreline for as long as anyone could remember. It was a huge piece of rock that tapered down to a tiny stand—a sculpture crafted by nature. It seemed to balance on that tiny stand in defiance of physics. People would take pictures of the rock and themselves in front of the rock. It was an indelible part of the coastline.

Then one hurricane came along, and it was just…gone. Wiped out. Erased.

Again, no one died but it was still sad and certainly a notable event.

A Twitter friend shared the news on their feed. They posted pictures of the before and after. It was quite something. I Quote Tweeted it with some commiseratory words about how even though no one had died, it was still pretty awful.

Later that evening, I saw a story about it on the news. It was at the end of the national newscast—again, *no one died*—but they did devote some time to it.

Pretty good coverage for a rock.

Then even later that evening I was scrolling through Twitter and saw a reply to my quote tweet about the former-rock formation. The tweeter stated that it was a disgrace that the MSM, as the rage-addicted and rage-farmers alike refer to mainstream media (they also like "Lamestream Media" but that's always seemed a little high school-ish to me...or maybe suggestive of prostate issues), hadn't covered the story.

The story I just watched. On National News. Which is just about as MSM as you can get.

So the issue was less about mainstream media not providing coverage to the things that matter but more to the point that this person wasn't watching so-called Mainstream Media.

It's been the battle cry of the pseudo-marginalized for years now that MSM is ignoring the "real" stories. You can only find the truth on...Facebook? YouTube? Twitter?

Ah yes, we all know about social media's rigorous fact-checking before allowing content on to their massive un-gated platforms (please read that sentence with your most sarcastic voice while rolling your eyes, it'll really bring it to life).

But this is where we are currently. Mainstream media, with all its legal accountability and real-world consequences for spreading false information, has suddenly become the bad guy. Not without some just cause. There's a lot to be suspicious of on your TV News...but maybe not so much when you have multiple unrelated TV News stations around the world reporting the same facts.

But let's not let MSM off that easy. In an effort to reach more people and ensure them that they ARE indeed covering that story about the big rock that fell down, they joined social media. Which, if you are disciplined and discerning, is great because you can easily get verifiable information from a mostly reliable source.

The sad news is, of course, that none of us have the time to be disciplined and discerning. We're all too busy scrolling to the next amazing video or hot take. We've become the media and we're wildly unreliable.

It's right there in the name. Social media. Social as in a bunch of people. Media as in "here's what happened to that big rock."

Right or wrong—and it's mostly wrong—we've become the "media." I'll even go as far as saying we've become the new mainstream media, or NMSM. We should make red hats.

The internet has always offered up some tasty confirmation bias. If you want to find someone to back up some crazy conspiracy theory you heard or even made up yourself, the internet has almost always got someone for you. Social media has just accelerated that by making every post feel equal.

Your crazy aunt's anti-vax post about how if you made the mistake of getting vaccinated, she's "found a home recipe for a poultice that will remove the harmful effects of the shot and all you have to do is throw that pungent ball in your underpants for a week" is sitting right above MSNBC's post about how getting vaccinated probably helped save your worthless life in the pandemic.

WHICH ONE IS RIGHT? They both occupy similar real estate on your screen. Your aunt's post seems a bit thrown together and contains multiple spelling errors but then again MSNBC's spelling is a little *too* good, don't you think?

Your aunt has become the new mainstream media. She only has local accountability but has global reach. Plus she did give you $50 on your birthday once.

The good news is, I think this won't last.

I think that actual MSM will be forced to remove itself from social media or, at the very least, demand segregation from the river of conspiratorial garbage and attempted comedy/vitriol.

I don't know when that will happen but I think it will happen sooner than you think.

But don't worry, your aunt will post about it when it happens.

FEED THE TROLLS (POISON)

SURVIVAL TIP: NOT ENGAGING IS POISON TO TROLLS. FEED THE TROLLS POISON.

I think it probably started back in the caveman days.

After a hard day of unsuccessful mammoth hunting, Grog was probably walking home past some other cavemen feeling a bit disappointed in himself, and Slog shouted out, "Great job on the mammoth hunt, Grog."

Funny, sure. Less so to Grog, but largely harmless dick-headery on the part of Slog. Classic Slog.

In our current day, it's like we decided to make Slog the president or head of a social media company. Somehow we've decided that the craft of trolling can be a stepping stone from the benign to the impactful. Actually, it's more a lateral move these days.

One of my favorite things about the online forum Reddit is the comments section. Each commenter competing with the last to post the funniest take on the original post, or even a take on another comment. It's a rough ride if you're the guy who made the content that everybody is ripping to shreds, but even then, you can see the comedic value in it.

But lately, it's been like we decided to take the author of the best worst comment and made them the boss of everything.

It's like if that class clown from high school who always had a smarmy comeback to the teacher or would make fart noises when the teacher bent over or would generally disrupt the class every day was suddenly in charge of education for the country.

We love to be entertained, but I think we're getting a little sloppy on where the line between entertainment and the importance of responsibility is. A pseudo-billionaire reality game show host was harmless to most of us. Just a curmudgeonly old man with seemingly lots of money who made rash decisions sometimes based on fact, sometimes based on his gut, and sometimes based on a jape. Then he'd look around the boardroom to his children and underlings for their nervous approval.

A pseudo-billionaire reality game show host with access to the nuclear codes was less harmless and less entertaining. More, what's the word? Horrific. Like giving the creepiest clown at the circus a gun.

So we've entered this weird age where we're supposed to be cool with the people in charge talking about how crap things are. That makes no sense and it starts to lose its funny real quick. Like a Reddit user trolling their own content by trying to come up with the pithiest comment. It's discount meta.

There's an anonymity online that I think is essential for some people. Abuse victims, political resistors (and no, that doesn't mean the "our own immunity is strong enough" crowd), and fans of Nickelback (I tease...Nickelback is great but their fans should probably be publicly outed in case one lives near you), all may want some anonymity at times. And that's fair.

Obviously, the ability to fire back your hottest take on something and not have any accountability is problematic.... However, the people who proudly take credit for those sometimes sketchy comments are even more problematic. The latter of those two has given rise to the notion of Professional Troll as career option. That's not good.

I understand it, but it's not good.

I understand it as a guy who makes videos about his hot takes that he hopes you occasionally find funny. There's power in trolling but mainly in trolling...power.

The problem begins when those who are trolls get to positions of power and keep on trolling. It's like none of them have even bothered to heed Uncle Ben's words of "With great power comes great responsibility." Did they even see Tobey Maguire's Spider-Man?

A president trolling the government is trolling himself. Funny, but isn't he the guy who's supposed to fix things?

A business owner who trolls his own business is, uh... trolling his own business. Again, funny, but aren't they the ones who should be fixing things?

When trolls get into positions of power and don't change their troll ways, it's like saying to your baby, "When's someone going to do something about that dirty diaper smell? This place smells like a fart had sex with a bag of curdled milk. Amirite?"

Your baby may or may not find that funny, depending on how developed their frontal lobe is and if you've exposed them to enough Norm Macdonald bits, but probably not if they're the one in the dirty diaper and you're the one in charge.

The good news is that silence that your baby would likely deliver in response is exactly the poison that is fatal to trolls.

You've likely heard the term "don't feed the trolls." This refers to getting in to a dialogue with the trolls and either attempting to chastise or tell them how offended you are, which becomes metaphorical food for the trolls, and the reason for the saying is that it if you feed them that food, they will continue to thrive.

Not engaging with trolls is like poison to them. The more you don't engage, the more poison you feed them, and they eventually die off.

Obviously, those in power need to be held accountable for their actions, but that is wildly different from engaging with something that is quite clearly them being a troll.

When they do that, do nothing. Feed the trolls...poison.

Politics Is Awful

WIZARD OF US

SURVIVAL TIP: WHEN A THIRD PARTY SUGGESTS THAT THE CAUSE OF YOUR PROBLEMS IS ANOTHER GROUP OF PEOPLE, THE REAL CAUSE MAY BE THEM.

It's so damn effective.

It's so damn effective, and it's so damn attractive.

The idea that your problems are not your own fault. The idea that you're being thwarted at every step by a group of "others." The idea that the only reason you haven't fully realized your potential is because some group of people won't let you. The idea that "they" are trying to keep you down.

Now, let's be clear. Unless you're white, straight, cisgender, middle-class, or upwards...you're probably right. There probably IS a group of people who want to impede any of your attempts at success. However, those people are easily classified as racists, bigots, homophobes, transphobes, and the like. There is no need to refer to them with a mysterious "they/them." Unless they're pronoun-phobic, then it's just fun.

But I'm referring to the more generalized "bogeyman" style of Us vs Them. The tactic used by politicians who usually have little else to offer. In the absence of a plan, present a foe.

People eat that stuff up and are usually eager to get behind something or someone when they feel threatened. Sometimes that's a good thing. If government suspends the right to strike, people get upset and they rally together to support the fight. That's a good thing. When a politician says the reason you can't get a good job is because of people with hazel eyes, that's a bad thing.

But damn it, it's continued to work through the ages. Despite us evolving to know better.

Of course, it makes sense from an evolutionary stance. According to psychological studies, babies who can't talk yet prefer other babies who look like they do.[1] Racist babies. Okay, maybe not racist babies. That Us vs Them makes sense from a socio-biological view. If you're a baby and you're hungry for mother's milk, you should probably aim for Mom and not the dog. You made that mistake once. He was NOT happy.

So, visual differences are at least understandable, and hopefully we grow out of that, based on the experience that skin color or appearance doesn't necessarily define a required division between us.

But we seem to have taken the Us vs Them mentality to the extreme. Applying it to the most indistinguishable "them" possible. Far beyond visual cues, we've waded into the ridiculous, like political affiliation or "left" and "right."

---

1 Neha Mahajan and Karen Wynn, "Origins of 'Us' Versus 'Them': Prelinguistic Infants Prefer Similar Others," *Cognition* vol. 124, 2 (2012), pp. 227-33, doi:10.1016/j.cognition.2012.05.003. https://pubmed.ncbi.nlm.nih.gov/22668879/

To be fair, I do realize there are political views that can be described as "left" or "right" but the idea that we all go to our respective meetings and work as a unit is laughable. I'm one good sandwich away from being gay and communist, and I've yet to be invited to a meeting of the "left." (That phrase is based on the fact that the majority of sandwich shops in our small town are owned by gay couples. I don't know if they're communists. I don't think so. Can gay people even be communists? Far be it from me to stop them though.)

It's a grift. A grift executed by lazy politicians who have their eye on power and nothing else. A grift implemented to use people and capitalize on times of uncertainty. A "listen, things are a bit weird right now, but we can all agree it's 'their' fault" ruse that only serves those who pronounce it.

More often than not, the politicians who use words like "gatekeeper" and "elite" are both of those things and have the paychecks, houses, cars, and support staff to prove it.

Red flags should be flung into the air at the first hint of Us vs Them. It's a sign that someone is exploiting very real fears and doing bugger all to actually address those fears. They just want the power, the money, and the trappings that go with it. They usually have no plan except for...more power, money, and trappings.

Of course, there are issues where there are, in fact, sides. There are issues where it's important to know who is "Us" and who is "Them." Like a woman's right to choose what happens with her own body versus a man's ability to somehow make that choice for her. However, a quick peek behind the curtain on those issues will most likely reveal a "Wizard of Us" (oooh, that's a better title, I'm changing it now) who is stoking the fires and spelling out potential consequences that further stoke the fires.

True leaders and good politicians aren't interested in dividing people into Us and Them. They want to offer a hand up to all. They want to offer an understanding ear and problem-solving to everyone for the good of everyone.

Yes, even stupid people who don't think like you.

I AM A (GROUCHO) MARXIST

SURVIVAL TIP: THE CORRECT ANSWER TO THE QUESTION, "ARE YOU RIGHT OR LEFT WING?" IS "I'M ACTUALLY VEGAN." THIS WILL PREVENT ANY FURTHER DISCUSSION AS THE PERSON WHO ASKED WILL RUN AWAY TO AVOID THE IMPARTING OF ANY "DELICIOUS" VEGAN RECIPES.

He looked me up and down with one eyebrow cocked and asked in a thick accent, "Whit team dae ye support?"

I had prepared for this. My wife, my then fiancée, had warned me this would be one of the first questions I would be asked when I started my new job at the Virgin Megastore in Glasgow, Scotland.

The teams in question played soccer/football. My choice was really between two teams. One traditionally Catholic (Glasgow Celtic) and one traditionally Protestant (Glasgow Rangers).

Sure, I could have said Clydebank FC, to whom I currently pay my £10/year membership dues to support (largely because they were once sponsored by the pop group Wet Wet Wet which was emblazoned on their shirts.... I mean, c'mon), but that would have likely resulted in me getting punched. Not immediately, but rather a "punch credit" that could be redeemed at a later date of the holder's choosing. Like say, after a couple of pints at the local pub.

No, I was prepared. I knew my answer would determine my fate for the rest of my career there. It would affect every single interaction, every single day.

I learned early in life that when faced with an impossible situation, the best action is "nonsense." When I say I learned this early in life, I mean I learned this by watching that episode of *Happy Days* where Richie Cunningham faces some thugs who want to fight. He starts jumping up and down and acting crazy, thereby making him more trouble than he was worth, and the thugs gave up on him.

It was reinforced many years later in a story from Sting told while he was working on his album *Nothing Like the Sun*. The title was the result of a run-in with a brute who wanted to punch him. To be fair to the brute, I'm sure many people throughout recent history have wanted to punch Sting. However, it's just not something you go around doing.

Faced with a pummeling, Sting pulled the ol' Richie Cunningham on the brute and decided to recite one of Shakespeare's sonnets with great assertion.

"My mistress' eyes are nothing like the sun;
Coral is far more red than her lips' red;
If snow be white, why then her breasts are dun;
If hair be wires, black wires grow on her head."

Not one of Will's most romantic works. It basically amounts to "she ain't much to look at, but she's mine." The important thing is it worked. It was not the expected exchange for the brute, and it made punching Sting look like more trouble than it was worth.

So, back to Glasgow...

"Whit team dae ye support?"

As said, I was ready.

"The Toronto Maple Leafs," I replied with a smile that suggested I was keen to talk about the Leafs.

He rolled his eyes and left the room...hopefully to inform the others that I was not worth the trouble of asking.

I feel this way about the "left" and "right." It's way too easy to stick a banner over a group of people and assume they all feel the same way about every issue because they happen to agree on one issue.

But that's humans for you, isn't it? Always assigning people into groups so you know who you should punch or hug.

I've always avoided pledging my allegiance to a group. It gets dodgy. If you're part of a group and someone in that group does something stupid, it's basically like you've done the stupid thing too. Or you at least think said stupid thing wasn't stupid at all.

Not for me. People are stupid. I'm stupid. I do enough stupid things on my own to start sharing responsibility for the stupid things other people do.

This is especially true for politics.

People rarely ask me if I'm "left" or "right." They assume I'm "left" leaning. Though I was once approached by a youngish man in a bar with the line "Judging by the way you dress, I'm assuming you lean politically to the 'right'?"

I haven't worn a sports jacket with a tucked in shirt since.

I like to think of myself as a Marxist. Not that kind. A Groucho Marxist. After Groucho Marx, who famously said, "I refuse to join any club that would have me as a member."

I realize this stance might make it seem like I am powerless in our current political world. Politics demands you take a side...but I think the opposite and I don't think it means I'm "undecided." I think that not pledging allegiance to an arbitrary club leaves me free to support the things I feel are important. It also denies others the ability to simply drop me into a category. They can't assume how I feel about specific issues.

I sometimes think I should start a new political wing for those who feel the same way...but then of course, I'd have to quit it.

POLITICS AND PROFESSIONAL WRESTLING

SURVIVAL TIP: DON'T WASTE YOUR TIME AND ENERGY HATING AWFUL POLITICIANS THAT INSULT OTHER AWFUL POLITICIANS. IT'S JUST PART OF THE SHOW.

There are many things I despise about politicians.

Not all politicians, obviously. Plus I think it's essential that we get as many new smart people into politics as possible. If only we could make politics less politicky. And by that, I mean less theatrical.

Imagine being a politician and having your opponent in an election say that your dad killed Kennedy and your wife was ugly…and then going for dinner with that opponent after the election WITH your wife. It beggars belief.

I can understand the rationale behind taking fairly light personal insults as part of the barbed repartee of politicking, but if someone brings in something you can't control like your looks or your family, I can't understand how you can just turn that off and then go have dinner together.

But politicians do that. They can stand across from each other and say the most hurtful things in a debate this week and then be applauding each other at a rally next week. It's a bit stomach churning. Especially these days when we are dealing with issues larger than just how to pay down the debt (important, surely, but not as urgent as other matters) and we get emotionally invested in our politicians. We put our own necks on the line and online in our support for them. We jeer their opponents and scream blue murder when they are unjustly attacked or insulted.

Then they go for dinner together.

And smile for the cameras.

Like they're freakin' best friends.

Then it dawns on you that while the issues are real—very real—the politicians are just characters in some sort of weird performance art.

I had a young woman explain her love of professional wrestling to me once. This sounds like the beginning of a joke or a fabricated sexy story but it is not, it's just about wrestling. She was unlike what you might expect a professional wrestling fan to be. Mid-20s, professional, very well-spoken and well-read. I'm not saying there aren't tons of professional wrestling fans like her, I'm just saying she isn't who jumps to mind when you envision people ringside screaming, "Hit him with the chair! Here! Hit him with MY chair!" But alas, she was indeed one of those people.

I questioned her on how she could be a fan of something so rigged and scripted and with outcomes planned far in advance based on a desired storyline and the story arc that will best suit the franchise. She smiled (and probably thought of putting me in a half nelson) and calmly explained that people watch the Super Bowl each year. Millions watch. Some years it's a thrilling game with a nail-biting finish…but most years it's kinda…*boring*. She went on to say that as a football fan, you roll the dice each game you watch. You have no idea if it will be entertaining.

With professional wrestling, every damn event is thrilling.

Every single event has villains and heroes and breathtaking, heart-stopping moments that keep you engaged.

Now, I'm not here to suggest that politics is staged, scripted, rigged, and with results planned far in advance based a desired storyline and story arc that will best suit the franchise. Sure, sometimes it feels that way and may be that way in some instances. However, there are too many franchises, and they all want to be Hulk Hogan (yes, I know that's an old reference) or Becky Lynch (See? I'm cool).

Sure, some of politics is sketchy and rigged, but not all of it. Too many people want that power. However, the comparison to professional wrestling is hard to squirm out of. Harder to squirm out of than a powerslam, piledriver, or another wrestling move that I just looked up on Google.

In a weird and disappointing way though, it's good that politics is so theatrical. With voter turnouts abysmally low in most places, I'm kind of in favor of anything that will get people's attention and get them involved. Sure, it gets creepy and hard to stomach sometimes but I'd much rather see people voting for things that are important to them instead of just assuming it doesn't matter if they pay attention or not. That's the real danger.

If that means getting a little too involved in your support of a politician and then being shocked and a little hurt when they shake hands with the person you've been treating as the villain in the story, so be it, I guess.

Just remember that the moves may look real, but they're all just part of the performance.

POLITICS SHOULD NOT BE ENTERTAINING

SURVIVAL TIP: SHOULD YOU FIND YOURSELF BEING ENTERTAINED MORE THAN ANGERED BY POLITICS, TAKE A BREAK AND ATTEMPT TO READJUST TO NORMAL SOCIETY.

Politics is usually about making non-immediate, and to a varying degree, life and death decisions.

Those decisions will form policies and laws that will guide society in a particular direction, and with that movement, society will experience the inevitable consequences of those policies and laws.

Its topics of debate are most often of vital importance to some segment of society.

For this reason, politics should not be entertaining.

Yet, millions of us ARE entertained by it. That's a problem.

We've somehow turned politics into a sport where winning power and holding on to it—not serving the public good—is the ultimate goal.

This is a terrible evolution for a noble concept that probably started with the best of intentions from the founders of politics like Plato, Confucius, and Chanakya saying, "Everyone's putting their garbage bins out willy-nilly...let's pick a day...a Garbage Day."

I'm not suggesting that politics should be boring.

Well, if I had to choose between entertaining and boring, I'd pick boring.

However, politics has become more about the politicians and less about the politics. That's not to say certain issues aren't still of massive importance to people, however it's getting more and more difficult to critique something political without it being assumed that you're waving a giant foam #1 hand for the opposing political party.

That's a problem.

I long for the days when it was us versus the government. When we could jointly be angry at governmental decisions without it being assumed that we're in total agreement with the next bunch of goof wads desperate to take power.

Politics has become cinematic. Actually, it's become positively two-dimensional.

Like it should be part of the Marvel Cinematic Universe. We've chosen to see politicians as "pure good" or "pure evil" because it's easier for us to consume and it makes us want to watch election coverage.

What kind of society have we become where we watch hours upon hours of election coverage...*for fun*?

I want to be clear. In the past six or so years, we have drifted beyond the policy-based differences and veered into some pretty serious issues that demand some serious attention.

However, I think we got here because of this push to turn politics into the WWE (see previous chapter). We gobble it up when the news channels, desperate for content to fill that twenty-four-hour news cycle, paint politicians as something less human and more cartoonish. It makes it easier to choose sides.

That's a problem.

Politicians are humans. Many, if not most, get into politics to serve the public in some capacity. They put themselves out there, which is incredibly bold, with the best of intentions… but then something happens.

They realize to see success they need clout, and to gain clout they need clicks and views, and to get clicks and views they need to strip away nuance and any grey areas and pick a side—black or white—and play that character to the exclusion of common sense and rational thought.

I get it. I love *Star Wars*. I love the battle between Light and the Dark side.

Am I willing to accept that some of Darth Vader's policies are actually pretty good?

I mean, he's generated a LOT of jobs in building that Death Star.

Will I admit that Luke Skywalker's treatment of the Ewoks is borderline racist?

He is rather condescending to them.

Well, that makes the whole story a bit more nuanced than I want.

Politics in real life is not *Star Wars*, despite any actual star warring that may be happening.

Politics in real life is not a TV show despite being on TV 24/7.

Politics is the very real business of attempting to make real life better for society (and yes, I know that means different things to different people).

Politics should not be entertaining.

Politicians should not be revered like celebrities because they're politicians.

Celebrity corrupts and twists and becomes entirely about maintaining celebrity.

I know this personally, even with my modicum of celebrity. Every time I get recognized at the grocery store, I feel good, so I walk around the produce section a few more times just to get recognized again.

Okay, that may not be entirely true but you get my point.

Politics should be similar to doing your taxes: a civil burden that deep down we know is good for us in the grand scheme of things, but dear god it's awful while you're in the thick of it.

I'm tired of political entertainment.

At best, it's poor theatre.

At worst, it's being entirely cavalier with people's lives.

Politics should be nuanced. Politics should be borderline boring.

But where's the fun in that, I guess?

THE BEST-LOOKING TEACHER PHENOMENA

SURVIVAL TIP: WHEN CHOOSING THE BEST OF THE BUNCH, IT'S INTEGRAL TO IGNORE OTHER BUNCHES.

Back in high school physics class, we had a student teacher take over the class for a month or so while our regular teacher sat at the back and did whatever people did before they killed time on their phones. (Crosswords? Contemplate life? How *did* people survive?)

The student teacher was quite young and dressed similar to how we students were *trying* to dress. Except it was evident that he had experience and a degree of finesse that only came with being twenty-four compared to us at fourteen.

He also had decent hair. A contemporary hairstyle (it was the '80s, so let's keep that in mind) with a noticeable mastery of hair products. He obviously had had some experience with Aqua Net or French Formula that far outpaced us teens.

Standing in comparison to our regular teacher in his worn-out cardigan, seen-better-days shirt and trousers, and shoes that were expensive when he bought them thirty years ago (btw, this is a sartorial style mostly unique to the teaching profession that exposes a steadily growing frugality over the years, whether justified or not), the student teacher looked like a new wave Adonis.

The girls in the class, and a few of the boys, were smitten. Even the boys who weren't interested in boys thought he was pretty damn cool. Never before had a group of fourteen- and fifteen-year-olds been so interested in the science of physics. Suddenly, students were asking for extra help on this or that chapter and wanted to make sure they were understanding this or that assignment clearly. Kids who would normally ask to go to the bathroom and then skip the class…weren't. They'd stay. For the whole class.

We'd see him in the halls, and we would compete to see who he would say "hi" to. Extra points if he said your name.

But then one day the smoke cleared and the mirrors were exposed. We all saw the truth. The horrible pedestrian truth.

It happened downtown.

Amongst a sea of faces, we recognized his. Out of context. Wide open to a larger comparison pool.

There he was, looking…we choked back a little bit of vomit and rubbed our eyes…normal. Not even that great for normal, to be honest. He was just…okay looking.

His clothes seemed less Duran Duran and more Dexys Midnight Runners.

His hair looked less Nick Rhodes and more Flock of Seagulls tribute band.

We wondered if something horrible had happened to him. Had he been in an accident that horribly deformed him down from chiseled to unremarkable? Had he been robbed by a thief who was now escaping with his ACTUAL cool clothes and left him with the run-of-the-mill guise he had on now?

We (probably) cried ourselves to sleep that night, feeling terrible for him and whatever fate had befallen him.

Then we returned to school the next day and he looked good again. Like, really good.

What was this magic? This transformation from cool to fool and back again?

Then it dawned on us. He was just the best looking teacher.

In an environment full of middle-aged and older tired and jaded schoolteachers, he looked exceptionally good.

However, out in the real world with a larger selection of people to compare with…he looked average at best.

Now, should that student teacher be reading this, there was nothing wrong with you. Your hair and clothes and general looks were nowhere close to offensive. It's just that they all looked better the closer you got to a bunch of old people who put "pride in appearance" further down the daily list.

Politics is very similar.

People often go on about how handsome JFK was. Was he? Was he really though? Or did he just seem really handsome standing next to Nixon?

People often say that Justin Trudeau is just a "pretty-boy." Is he? Is he really though? Or does he just look that way in the context of who else is in government?

Not saying this to take away anything about the appearances of either man. They were, and are, fine looking people.

But beyond the physical appearance, this is how politics works.

We are forced to choose the "best looking teacher" at school, even though we know they'll be reduced to mere flawed mortals if we see them in the context of the rest of the world. We choose the politicians whose policies and platforms are the closest to what we would like to see happen, even though we know that in comparison to a myriad of alternatives they may not be as appealing.

Some people can even convince themselves those policies and platforms are the best looking policies and platforms they've ever seen. This, of course, is delusional and absolute nonsense. Sure, some parts may be good but they're only the best of the available bunch.

So, what's to be done about this?

Well, being aware that we may only be picking the best-looking teacher at school probably helps remind us that there is probably better out there, and hopefully that makes us strive for better.

Better politicians, not better looking teachers.

MIDDLEWORD

BY MARY TRUMP, PHD

A Middleword?
Are you fucking serious?
What even is that?
Ryan, call me.

—Mary Trump

Marriage Is Wonderful

(my wife may read this)

HONESTY IS OVERRATED

SURVIVAL TIP: THERE CAN BE NO SECRETS IN A MARRIAGE EXCEPT FOR ALL THE ONES THAT NEED TO BE KEPT SECRET.

I have never cheated on my wife.

Either of them.

My first wife cheated on me, but that all worked out for the best as I was able to trade up to a "younger, leggier model." Those aren't my words (the "younger, leggier model" bit). They're the words of a person I know who also got divorced... but as the guy who was cheated on, I like them, they fit, and they're accurate. It feels like, even though I was the guy who was given the short end of the stick, I still won. And I did.

There is a popular notion that there can be no secrets in a successful marriage.

This is wrong.

For a successful marriage, there must be some secrets.

I'm not talking about the big stuff like having an affair or losing your job and the like. No, those are not good secrets to keep. Those are secrets that threaten to detonate bombs at the foundation of a successful marriage.

I'm referring to other secrets. Secrets of convenience. Secrets of pleasantry. Secrets of "I don't know what I'm doing yet."

Secrets of convenience are simple secrets—the type of secrets that expedite regular boring life. For example, not telling your spouse how expensive the leaf blower that you bought was because it's way faster than raking, it's super fun to use, and you feel a little bit like you're in *Star Wars*. Plus, she comments on how nice the yard is looking and why would you potentially ruin that by getting into to a debate on the cost-effectiveness of various yard appliances you purchased over the years? It's a can of worms no one needs to open.

Secrets of pleasantry are those secrets that really have no benefit in being exposed. My wife, Shannon, has never seen me pedicure myself and she never will. She doesn't even know when I do it and where exactly. It is a secret I will take to the grave. I will continue to simply arrive with well-maintained feet and the magic of marriage will continue on.

Secrets of "I don't know what I'm doing just yet" are more vague. These are the things you are trying or experimenting with as potentially personality changing...like listening to all of Taylor Swift's new album by yourself in the car and wondering to yourself, "Will my spouse still accept me if I go full Swiftie?" There's no rush. You need to take time to figure out who you are.

Complete honesty in a marriage is something that people who've just broken up say is essential, or people who have never actually been married say is the goal.

They're wrong.

No one needs to know everything. Especially your spouse.

Again, I'm not talking about the big stuff. Cheating on your spouse is not a good secret to keep. It's by nature destructive to your marriage. Spending all of the money in your joint account is not a good secret to keep, and anyway, leaf blowers are less than a hundred bucks and won't bankrupt us and it's not a big deal at all.

Each secret must be weighed for its own value. Does keeping it protect the relationship? Does keeping it protect the feelings of your significant other?

The easy way to determine if a secret is best kept is imagining if the secret were revealed to your partner. Would knowing the secret call into question the relationship itself? Or would it just be gross or uncomfortable?

Remember, to have a successful marriage, your spouse has to live with you. Every day. For the rest of their life. At least that's the plan. So why wreck the show for them? Keep some mystery. Some secrets are necessary and serve a greater good.

It's a rookie mistake for newlyweds to say they must have no secrets. Thankfully, there is a quick and easy way to learn the value of keeping some secrets for new couples.

A quick stay at a hotel with one of those sliding barn door bathrooms.

Nothing will convince them of the joy and value in keeping some things secret from each other than the cavernous and echoing hard surfaces of a hotel bathroom that is barely separated from the rest of the room by a big stupid gaping barn door. A door that allows free travel for all sounds, scents, and delights. A romantic mood can dissipate as quickly as a puff of gas or three. Words of love can be drowned out by the heralding trumpets of reality.

A cruel and harsh but necessary lesson.

Yes, some secrets are worth keeping secret…for the good of the relationship.

MARRIAGE IS LIKE WORKING IN A HOTEL

SURVIVAL TIP: DISCRETELY ANTICIPATING NEEDS CAN MAKE ANY RELATIONSHIP FEEL LIKE A FIVE-STAR EXPERIENCE.

I used to work in a hotel.

It was a twenty-one room boutique hotel in a former mansion that was furnished with lots of antiques. Some very old. For example, one of the tables used for breakfast service in the lounge was from 1710. It still looked pretty good even with the coffee cup rings and plate scratches.

Everything was intentional and everything was put to work.

When I started as a front desk clerk, I learned fairly quickly that the more I anticipated guests' needs, the happier they were, and more importantly, the easier my job got.

I referred to this as "The Show" and here's how it went…

The entrance to this former mansion now hotel was a long hallway and the front desk was at the very end of the hallway. As soon as guests entered, their eyes were drawn down that hallway to...me. It felt right. It felt like preparation for people watching me on their phones while they were on the toilet.

Guests would enter through the double doors at the front of the building. I could hear them coming before they got to those doors so I would stand up from my chair behind the front desk. I would ease my face into a gentle smile and try to look welcoming and at the ready in an olde world hospitality style, you know, as opposed to a "commission sales staff in an electronics store" style.

"Good afternoon," I would project down the hallway. "Checking in?"

They weren't always checking in, some came to check the price, some came to meet someone else that was already staying there, but this was a solid way to start a conversation that immediately made the person feel welcome and let them know it was assumed that they belonged in this seemingly fancy establishment.

Once the guest was checked in, I would ask them if they required me to make any reservations for them for dinner at a local restaurant. It was an offer that said "let me take this one thing off your plate and make you look hella important."

Then, if they did go ahead with allowing me to make dinner reservations, I'd step it up a notch.

I'd call and order a taxi for ten to fifteen minutes prior to their reservation (or whatever time they'd need to leave in order to arrive in time for their reservation).

As the hotel was quite small and old, you could hear when room doors opened and closed from the front desk. The guests would make their way down the stairs, dressed and polished for a night out, and then make their way to the front desk where I would be standing waiting.

I would address the guest by name in a greeting and they would ask me if I could call a taxi for them.

"It's waiting for you outside, <insert guest name>," I would reply with a smile and a hint of "why would you debase yourself so much to think that there WOULDN'T be a taxi waiting for you?"

The guest would invariably be slightly taken aback but then thank me and head out the door.

Annnnd scene.

That was "The Show." Which amounted to "pretend you work in a nice hotel."

Which brings me to this...marriage is like working in a hotel.

As someone who has worked in a hotel, I feel bad behavior on the part of the guests is the result of a tone set by the workers of the hotel. Just like I think bad behavior on the part of people in marriages is a tone set by the workers in a marriage.

No, seriously...hear me out.

Like marriage, working in a hotel can be awful. People are demanding, messy, they leave their towels in a ball on the floor, they can forget they're married to someone else, etc.

I feel that kind of behavior can be curbed by those who are working in hotels by pretending they're working in a nice hotel and by those in marriages by pretending they're working in a nice marriage.

It's true. The same basic tricks work in both. I mean, I'm not suggesting the secret to a happy marriage is to trick your spouse, but also that's exactly what I'm saying.

Let me explain...

Bad hotels—and they don't have to be cheap to be bad—have staff that don't listen.

It's all reaction-based and transactional. Zero magic.

Actually listening to what guests are saying gives you many insights in to what they want, need, and desire.

It reduces your workload if you can plan ahead and anticipate those wants, needs, and desires.

Plus, it makes you feel like you're in a really good hotel... and it may be all that's required to actually BE a really good hotel.

Bad marriages have people that don't listen.

It's all reaction-based and transactional. Zero magic.

Actually listening to what your spouse is saying gives you many insights in to what they want, need, and desire.

It reduces your spousal workload if you plan ahead and anticipate those wants, needs, and desires.

Plus, it makes it feel like you're in a really good marriage...and it may be all that's required to actually BE a really good marriage.

Just like bad hotels, bad marriages provide the basic amenities, like a place to sleep, a place for your stuff, and towels that have seen better days and aren't that excited to see you naked, don't do a lot of maintenance, are maybe run down, skip the special touches like fluffing your pillows or keeping your coffee hot, and barely acknowledge the guests.

Good marriages, like good hotels, also have those pancake machines where you get to watch your pancake being made. This may not be a requirement for a good hotel or marriage, but if my wife reads this, it totally is, and I really want her to listen to this want/need/desire of mine.

MARRIAGE IS, YOU KNOW, WITH THE...

SURVIVAL TIP: THE KEY TO A SUCCESSFUL MARRIAGE OR RELATIONSHIP IS EVOLVING YOUR COMMUNICATION TO AN INDEXICAL LEVEL AS SOON AS POSSIBLE.

At the beginning of a relationship, there is a focus on language.

The words you say to each other *before* you get married and it gets legally difficult for your spouse to leave are very important. You want to strike a balance between tenderness and clarity. Nothing should be left to guessing. Intent should be spelled out. Consent should be crystal clear.

Communication is vital. This was my biggest takeaway from watching *Three's Company* as a kid. If Jack, Chrissy, or Janet didn't explicitly state what they were doing, hijinks would ensue, the Ropers would be livid, and drinks would be thrown at the Regal Beagle.

Of course, it is essential to communicate and communicate well. It steers you clear of misunderstandings and heartache. It allows each person in any relationship—whether it be passing, commercial, platonic, or romantic—to know where they stand. So they can move on with their day and/or return to staring blankly at their phone.

However, marriages and long-term relationships are different. Sometimes more words mean more problems. They can become a sticky web of detail that is nigh impossible to shake free from. Too many words can cloud intent and can even suggest deception. They can fold back over into themselves and muddy the waters instead of making them clearer. This is no good for any relationship that wishes to survive in the long run.

Conversation in relationships that wish to survive should ideally evolve to be more like this…

"Hey, do you?"

"With the?"

"Well…"

"I did the…"

"Oh, good."

"Yeah?"

"Yeah."

Completely indexical.

Like a secret language that you and your partner have created over time and you're in so deep that you're only one stop short of telepathic. A conversational rhythm that is akin to a record skipping wildly…or for those who are younger than fifty, a mobile phone call on a phone that is only getting 3G service while you're at the very back of Costco.

This, I believe, is the sign of a successful relationship. You have distilled interrelationship communication to its essence.

My wife, Shannon, and I have had many serious conversations entirely devoid of any nouns. We have negotiated chores with three gestures, four grunts, and a fart (mine). We have waxed poetic in a romantic moment with only the words "eh?" "pizza pocket," and "Tylenol."

But it wasn't easy. Getting to this stage of indexical communication requires practice and so much trial and error. There was many a time I would say something perfectly clear like "Should?" and she would misunderstand that as commentary about what she was having to drink or eat at the time when it was obvious I was asking her if we should move the oil change for the car from next Wednesday to Friday because I have that thing and she's going to be doing that other thing in the place.

But don't fret. It will come eventually.

I would advise any couples looking to advance their relationship to the indexical communication level to take it step by step. Start by removing superfluous words like "and," "the," and "dishwasher." From there you can move on at your own pace to removing nouns, adjectives, and most consonants.

The benefit of being with someone in a long-term relationship is that they already know what you think, what you're thinking, and what you're going to think. So why waste time and effort on eloquence and loquaciousness when you already know the thing...with the...and the other.

An added unexpected bonus to indexical communication with your long-term partner is practically guaranteed fidelity.

It's true.

Once a relationship has reached the indexical communication point, each person is almost guaranteed to never stray.

This is primarily because no one else will understand them.

Sure, each person in a relationship can still communicate with others who they are not in a relationship with, but that is very different from any potential romantic dalliance that will require communicative clarity lest someone puts something somewhere that the other person was not expecting it to be put.

For example,

"Is?"

"What are you saying?"

"With?"

"What are you talking about?"

"Honk?"

"I have no idea what you're asking m...oh my god, did you just honk your boob in my ear?!"

In a long-term relationship, that conversation would have read like an erotic novel but in a new relationship, it's more likely to make the other person wonder if you're feral.

Indexical communication only works if the person you indexically communicate with knows what you're indexically referring to. That only comes with time.

So reap the rewards of your long-term love with the... maybe...hand soap...won't...of course...bins? ...Again? Too.

YOUR CHILDREN OR YOUR LOVE LIFE

SURVIVAL TIP: ENJOY MAKING YOUR CHILDREN, IT COULD BE THE LAST TIME YOU EVER ENJOY SEX.

I need to start with a warning here.

I am the proud father of two amazing adult sons, Owen and Gregor. If you are either of these people, please don't read this until I'm dead so that we can look each other in the eye until then.

Are they gone? Okay, let's continue with our filthy business.

See? I could probably stop writing right there. Your love life and your children cannot co-exist. At least not easily.

For most, your love life is an integral part of your relationship with your significant other prior to having children. It's how you make your feelings tangible and sometimes ticklish. It is a way for you to share something with another human that you do not and cannot share with another human.

I'm not talking about just sex. That's perfunctory and not always tied to emotion.

I'm talking about your love life. Your romantic nomenclatures for each other's bits and pieces. Your love life before you have children is a viable plan for the evening.

For example...

"What do you want to do tonight?"

"How about each other?"

Your love life is exciting and fulfilling and packed with throbbing intent...but then you have children.

That's how biology gets ya.

It keeps you all fired up and focused on procreation, and then suddenly out of nowhere for some goddamn reason you end up procreating.

If you're lucky, of course.

But suddenly your love life goes from walking around your home starkers together or snuggling up starkers under a blanket to watch a movie or enjoying a glass of wine starkers or doing your taxes starkers—my point being, you do a lot of things naked together before you have kids—to suddenly being acutely aware of the shame for your filthy lust for a basic human need.

There are, as I've read, parents who continue their nakedness even after they have children, but those people are weirdos.

Upon having children, your love life becomes a secret activity that no one should know about. This does, at first, heighten the "Ooh! we're so naughty" aspects of your love life but that is soon overtaken by "Did I just hear one of the kids get out of bed??" and/or "The baby's crying, get that out of my face."

Once you have children, your love life immediately is up for truncating and distilling down to the most efficient and least satisfying version of itself. It becomes goal based. Like a chore that briefly feels good. The emotion is still there but it has transformed special magic time into something more akin to mowing your lawn if you never wanted your children to know you mowed your lawn. You have to do it every now and then and you actually enjoy it when you can take your time, but now you have to do it super-fast so you don't get caught by your kids.

And you will get caught by your kids.

Again, Owen and Gregor, I swear to god you better not have read this far.

I feel confident that every single child on the earth throughout history has walked in on their parents...uh, mowing the lawn.

I also feel confident that every single child on the earth throughout history has suppressed that memory and we probably shouldn't dwell on that thought for too long because "Mommy's not hurting Daddy he's very happy right now and oh my god get out get out get out!"

.

.

.

Sorry, blacked out for a second there.

It is one of life's crueler jokes that the primary purpose of your love life is also its downfall. I realize that initially seems like a very heterosexual perspective, but children don't care if you're gay or straight. They just want to ruin your love life. It's a sport for them.

Don't believe me? Ask anyone who's had kids.

As soon as your plans for a romantic weekend away to... uh, mow your lawns...is heard by your children, they immediately get to work on ruining things for you. You could have organized babysitting with their grandparents, booked a great non-refundable deal on a swanky hotel and spa, preened and plucked yourself to perfection, and as soon as your kids get wind of your plans, they begin licking handrails and sharing snacks with the kid in their class who ALWAYS has a snot rope hanging out of his nose, and as if on cue, the day before your escape to salvage what romance you have left in your relationship, they come down with a fever or start blowing chunks of what looks like cottage cheese all over the couch and your plans are obliterated.

No one warns you, but I am now.

It's your children or your love life. Pick one.

Then go mow your own lawn.

MARRIAGE IS A TAG TEAM SPORT

SURVIVAL TIP: WHEN LIFE HAS YOU ON THE ROPES, TAG YOUR SPOUSE IN.

Marriage isn't for everyone.

I get that and I understand but I can't imagine how hard it would be to go through life on your own. Everyone needs a support network. Whether that be family or friends. I guess there are lots of ways you can lean on others without being married...but this is the section about marriage. So, let's focus on that. Those other people can write their own damn book.

One of the things I learned about being in a good marriage that I didn't know prior to being married is that marriage is a tag team sport. If life is beating you up, you can simply reach out to tag your spouse and they'll step into the ring while you recharge. If you get overwhelmed, you can lean on them. If you feel down, they'll stay up. If you get sick, they'll do their best to carry your weight (not literally...well, maybe).

It's not about being codependent. That suggests more of a house of cards type set-up where if one of you stops supporting the other you both fall. That's not it at all. No, being in a successful tag team means you are each at your best so that if one of you goes down, the other one can step in.

My first experience with this was actually before Shannon and I got married. We had just started living together and we were still very young. I preface the story with that as a caveat or explanation for my stupidity in this story.

The weather was beautiful that summer and we headed to Shannon's family's cottage, which was made available to us for a few days. It's a gorgeous little cottage that was hand-built by Shannon's grandfather in the 1950s and looks out over a quiet, small, spring-fed lake.

In an effort to impress my young girlfriend, I stripped down as far as I could and began to soak up the sun.

There are two things you should know about this act that I know now, and I knew then but apparently chose to ignore because I am an idiot. One, I am no Adonis. I have the body of a freakishly large three-year-old except hairier. That's right. The little belly, the shoulders that haven't fully grown in yet, and a massive head. Two, I have a sun allergy. I am literally allergic to the sun. Not severely, but enough so that I burn easily and my nerve endings turn into live wriggling electric worms under my sunburnt skin (at least, that's what it feels like).

I thought nothing of my time gorging on some Vitamin D and UV rays until it was too late. Suddenly, I was severely aware of the skin on my back and shoulders. Then the itch started, and the electric worms sprung to life. It was painful and awful and thankfully has only happened twice in my life. Then, and inexcusably, when I was fourteen in Florida with my parents and sister, and they had to determine what to do with a screaming maniac with a quickly blistering back.

But back to the cottage. My attempts at "sexy" were now replaced with "crazy huge-headed toddler in apparent severe discomfort." It was determined that a trip to the hospital was needed, and it was then that I discovered the beauty of a tag team relationship.

Shannon took control. She prepared our belongings and drove me to the nearest hospital...which was an hour and a half away.

I tagged her in, and she took over. She also didn't leave me the next day, for some unknown reason.

Our tag team relationship has demonstrated its benefit many, many times since then. From job worries to money worries, from parenting worries to family worries, we've been able to tag each other in when we need help.

Countless times when our kids were sick when they were little, one of us would work while the other took care of them. When that person was burning out, we'd tag the other person and swap roles.

It's truly wonderful and I'm so thankful for it. Again, I don't know how anyone could get by without having someone there to tag in.

Like when I got Covid this summer at that same cottage and Shannon had to drive my aged crumbling body, now like a melting gelatinous pumpkin version of my freakishly large three-year-old body but hairier, six hours back home while I shivered on the backseat under a sleeping bag before she too inevitably came down with it as well.

But I kept my shirt on this time.

The longer I stay married, the more I appreciate being married. I'm not sure what that means or says about myself or Shannon, but I'll take it and as we grow and mature, we know that we're there for each other if we stumble and need someone to tag in.

America Is a Nice Idea

AMERICA IS A CANDY STORE RUN BY TODDLERS WITH GUNS

SURVIVAL TIP: APPRECIATE AMERICA FOR WHAT IT IS BUT STICK TO THE GOOD BITS.

Remember when you were a kid and you would go to that one friend's house who gave you a full can of pop and a Twinkie when you asked for a drink and a snack? Whereas when your friends came to your house and asked for a drink and a snack they'd get a glass of tap water and maybe a cheese slice?

America is like that friend's house. At least from a Canadian perspective.

That friend's house was always fun to visit. More sugar than you could dare dream of, and when you got into your later teens, their parents would turn a blind eye when someone brought out a bottle of some horrible schnapps...peach or mint, but honestly, soon to be barf.

Initially it felt great but then that one time you were there and their mom, who had been schnapping a little too much herself, started to tell you she's noticed how much you've turned into a handsome young man. It initiated a host of disturbing thoughts. Was I ready to be my friend's new dad? It was too much.

You had now learned the lesson that your friend's house, while fun to visit, felt a little wild. A little lawless. It was perhaps a little too debaucherous for your tap water tastes and processed cheese slice palette.

This is what it is to be Canadian next to the world's sugariest superpower.

So much of the United States is tantalizing to those of us in the land of Peace, Order, and Good Government. That's Canada's answer to the US's "Life, Liberty, and the Pursuit of Happiness," by the way. No, really, it is. And now that you know this, it will make so much make so much sense.

Canadian popular culture is soaked in all things American. As Canadians, our ideas of success and excitement are defined by what we've seen in American movies. To the point that I was more excited to be at the White House (I was invited there by the Obama's.... BOOM, namedrop! I've been invited for the arrival ceremony of Prime Minister Trudeau...but that's another story) than I have ever been to be at the Parliament buildings in Ottawa. Not because of any reverence for the politics of the United States but because I'd seen the White House in countless movies and on TV. It's famous.

To be completely honest, the US has an abundance of awesomeness. Culturally, geographically, socially, and more.... From our snow-covered abodes up here in the sleepy north, it's easy to be bedazzled by all that the United States offers.

In fact, I take back my earlier analogy of America being like that one friend's house.

It's more than that.

It's a bit like being a toddler and living next to the biggest candy store in the world.

Except the candy store is also run by toddlers.

And they all have guns.

Of course, I'm exaggerating with this analogy. Well… kinda. About two people a week are shot by toddlers in the United States apparently. Anyway…

America loves America.

America loves America like a toddler loves candy. They know that they've got a good thing, they love it, and they want to suck it down to the stick.

Don't believe me? Take a trip to the Museum of US History in Washington, DC. They've been collecting and displaying every artifact of every part of United States history since George Washington (probably) said, "You know what? I think the King of England is a bit of a dick."

In fact, they have the uniform Washington was wearing when he (probably) said that.

Standing at the Washington Monument, you have unfettered sight lines to the Capitol Building, the Lincoln Memorial, and the White House. Like…they thought of that from the start. Canada would have just put them all next to each other, possibly even in the same building that would double as a bingo hall on Saturdays.

Right from the get-go, America has been aware of how good they've got it…and that's what makes America what it is.

America loves America.

Generally, that's a good thing. Confidence could almost entirely be regarded as an American invention.

Canada does not love Canada the same way.

Canada loves Canada like a toddler loves pants. Useful, sometimes pleasing, and largely required.

Though, much like a candy store run by candy-loving toddlers, there is possibly such a thing as too much of a good thing in America.

For the most part, living in the candy store means never having to look wistfully at the pants store next door and wishing you had all those pants. Whereas us here in the pants store often catch ourselves gazing longingly in the window of the candy store. Let's be clear, most of us Canadians love visiting the candy store.

They have everything there. All the stuff we can't get at home.

All the stuff that isn't necessarily...necessary. Or good for us.

But it's so great to visit. But we also love getting home.

It's true. Check the faces of fellow travelers returning to Canada from a winter vacation down south. Some may be less than enthusiastic...but almost all of them will smile when the Canada Border Services Agent says the iconic "Welcome home" as we trundle past with our bags from the candy store.

AMERICALAND

SURVIVAL TIP: REMIND YOURSELF EVERY NOW AND THEN ABOUT WHAT AMERICA WAS AIMING FOR BY VISITING WASHINGTON, DC.

America is a nice idea.

However, in the words of the immortal Gord Downie of The Tragically Hip, let me debunk an American myth and take my life in my hands.

The America that is mythologized is rarely the America that actually exists.

Except in Washington, DC.

To be clear, what follows is the perspective of someone who doesn't live in Washington, DC, so though there may be lots of terrible things about Washington, DC, this may be a very rose-colored glasses take.

But then again, so is any take on Disney World.

As a tourist, Washington, DC, like Disney World, hides its ugly innards well. Us tourists aren't generally aware of the bowels of the machine where they make glittering Americana and churros.

As a proud Canadian, I've never wanted to be American. I appreciate what America is trying to do but I've never been taken in by the "American Dream." I didn't even understand what it was. That is, until I visited DC.

Washington, DC, is the best of America. It's grand and oversized and magical and regal without being monarchistic in any way. Washington, DC, is like someone took the American Dream and made a theme park based on it.

Washington, DC, is Americaland.

Again, I understand that there are more than likely lots of horrible and sad parts to Washington, DC, but just like the four lane highways that exist for the garbage trucks under Disney World, we tourists don't see that bit.

We tourists see the impressive White House, the apparently almost siege-able Capitol Building, the Lincoln Memorial, and more. And then our minds are blown when someone points out that you can see all of those things when you stand at the Washington Monument. Like, the sightlines are clear. Completely intentional. Completely like a theme park.

And when you stand there looking down these sightlines, you can't help but think, "America is freaking amazing and maybe the happiest place on Earth!"

Then you take a walk down the National Mall and pop into the National Museum of American History and it's packed with the things you've grown up with as almost fairy tales but...they're real and they're right in front of you. From civil rights to celebrity. Like the Greensboro Lunch Counter is just...there. Dorothy's ruby slippers from *The Wizard of Oz* are...right there in front of you.

America does a number of things well, but its strongest skill is celebrating itself and its history. If you doubt that, just think of any national sporting event where America is involved. Invariably, chants of "U-S-A! U-S-A!" will be heard. I mean, it works well because it's three syllables but so is CA-NA-DA and we don't do it. This isn't a criticism. Hardly. It's to be commended. It's like willing national confidence into existence by sheer will.

What's really amazing about America's ability to celebrate itself and its history is that right from the get-go, Americans were like, "Put that somewhere safe. Because we're pretty cool and we need future generations to know that we've known that from the start."

For example, the National Museum of American History has a ton of cool stuff in it. Like, so much that you're at risk of missing all the cool stuff they have. On a recent trip, I entered an exhibit area and turned around to sidestep some people. I was facing a corner that I had completely missed upon entering, and there was George Washington's blue and gold outfit. The one you see him in in his portraits. The one that people wear fake versions of for Halloween. It was just...there. So even back in 1799, while America was still barely its own country, some early American who understood the assignment said, "Hey, bummer that George is dead, but before you give his stuff away to eighteenth-century Goodwill, can we keep his blue and gold outfit? Yeah, the fancy one everyone knows."

This is the sort of thing America does very well. It mythologizes itself.

Of course, America, like almost everywhere on the planet, has its problems. The middle class is disappearing, poverty is rampant, crime is a serious issue, many politicians have gone completely crazytown bananapants, the cost of living is sky-high, and some Americans are forced to choose between paying for their mortgage or their medical bills (seriously, America, figure out single-payer universal healthcare; all you're currently doing is making very rich health insurance companies even richer).

However, America remains to be known as the land of opportunity and that's still kinda right. In the same way that Disney World has Tomorrowland. It's less of a real place and more of a nice goal to aim for.

EVERYONE THINKS THEY'RE GOING TO BE RICH

SURVIVAL TIP: ASSUME YOU WILL NEVER BE RICH, THEN ANY WINDFALL, NO MATTER HOW SMALL, WILL BE BETTER APPRECIATED.

"Classic Eagle. 3:15. Thirsk."

My friend, Alan, who uttered those fateful words almost thirty years ago always asks me to shut up and tells me to "let it go" when I repeat them back to him.

Which I have essentially every single year since then. It's a great birthday message tradition.

We had been planning a trip to a pub called the Drovers Inn by Loch Lomond. Shannon and I had been living in Scotland for about a year, and we had discovered that there were services you could hire that would provide a driver and a van that would fit twelve people AND they would drive you two hours north to a pub in the middle of nowhere, wait until you drank yourself silly, and then safely return you to your home. They did all this for a measly £65.

We did not have £65. We had £10.

Alan arrived at our flat after his work shift and we told him the plan and the obstacle in our way. He looked at us with a twinkle in his eye and spoke forth those magical words: "Classic Eagle. 3:15. Thirsk." Once we determined he was intentionally making those sounds with his mouth and they were in fact actual words, he explained that he had been on the train home after work and at one stop the train conductor saw another train conductor on the platform. After a brief greeting, the train conductor on the platform bellowed out, "Classic Eagle. 3:15. Thirsk." and pointed to a newspaper which was folded to the horse racing information.

Aha! It was a bet. Classic Eagle: the horse. 3:15: the time of the race. Thirsk: the track.

Then Alan continued and told us that he had looked it up on the remaining journey and found out that if Classic Eagle won, it would pay 12 to 1 odds. A small £5 bet would yield £60. Which would bring us to the exact amount needed for our driver and van (we kept our booze money separate because we were financially responsible, and we really liked booze).

Off Alan and I went to the bookies to place our bet with only minutes to spare.

It should be noted that betting shops are perfectly legal in the UK, much like Tim Horton's and cannabis shops in Canada. Just one more way for you and your money to part ways but feel pretty good about it…at least momentarily.

We swam through the cigarette smoke and hopeful, but depressed, customers and placed the bet.

Then we watched the race.

We cheered for Classic Eagle as it sprang forth from the starting block or gate or whatever they call it.

We kept cheering as it fell behind.

We cheered less as it was now at the back of the pack.

We left quietly when it came in last.

We abandoned our plans for the van and driver and 400-year-old Scottish pub and instead satisfied our evening with some cheap store brand beer from the grocery store.

America is like that moment of hope we had when our plan was hatched, and we were already choosing seats in the van. We thought it was only a matter of time or technicality before we had all the money we wanted. Okay, the bare amount of money required.

I see a lot of that in America. This notion that any day now, your horse will win.

In some ways it's a great thing. It's hope. It's a way to keep trying and motivation to keep going and get up in the morning because any day now your ship will come in.

It also lets Americans celebrate the success of others. This is an almost uniquely American skill. Canada, like the UK and others, has a harder time celebrating the success of others.

There's an old saying that says that when a limousine drives through the poorest part of a city in America, the kids all cheer, point, and say, "That's going to be me someday!" When a limousine drives through the poorest part of a city in Canada, the kids point and say, "Who do they think they are?!"

Of course, it's not a hard and fast maxim, but it's a good generalization.

Americans are positive they're going to be rich any day now. They vote to give billionaires tax breaks because, I believe, they have this subconscious belief that they will be billionaires someday and they don't want to have to pay too much in taxes someday (to be fair, I think it's also because they celebrate success in general).

In other ways, it's not so great.

When the man who ended up being the 45th President of the United States ran for office, numerous stories emerged about how he had only paid a percentage of invoices for work done for him and his buildings. He had gained an alleged reputation of keeping his money by simply not paying his bills… to the detriment of those he worked with.

Yet still, he had, and has, many, many supporters who all think that if they can get close enough to him, that will somehow make them rich too. Ignoring the many, many warnings because they will only stand to gain, right?

There must be a balance that can be struck though. Somewhere between complete belief of wildly unlikely riches and a total abandonment of hope.

Somewhere between when Classic Eagle took off like a rocket and then fizzled like a slow horse.

VOTING IS TOO EASY

SURVIVAL TIP: WHENEVER YOU ARE GIVEN THE CHANCE TO VOTE, DO IT. DO IT FOR THE SIMPLE REASON THAT IT IS ALMOST GUARANTEED THAT SOMEONE DUMBER THAN YOU IS ALSO VOTING.

It was right before the 2016 US presidential election.

I was sitting on a bar patio in Anaheim, California, with some friends and we were discussing the absurdity of possibly electing Donald Trump as president. Actually, we weren't even considering it a possibility. It was a ludicrous hypothetical.

Everyone was aware of stories about him. We had seen the news. He was immensely entertaining as a benign TV character, but it seemed obvious that he wasn't an ideal choice for public office. There was no way you could imagine him wanting to "serve the people."

We laughed at the thought and were about to move on, when another friend who had walked up mid-conversation spoke.

"They shouldn't let everybody vote."

The rest of us at the table were shocked. We thought he MUST be joking, or we had accidentally been served Canadian beer with actual alcohol percentage. We demanded clarification that he was in fact joking.

Nope. He doubled down.

"Most people are too stupid to vote."

How could he say that?! It seems inherent that the right to vote exists for all in a democratic country. Especially the United States of America. Right?

His words actually offended me and the others at the table. We laughed but it was the laugh of those who can't believe they've had to listen to something so egregious.

We pressed him to explain himself. He spoke with a slight panic in his voice and told us that too many people don't know who or what they're voting for. That they base their vote on bad information or, worse, no information.

That didn't seem that big of an issue. There are always going to be uninformed voters. But that doesn't mean we should stop people from voting. Right?

"No," he continued, "but there are more and more of them every day."

Who is "them," we wondered aloud.

"People who don't think it matters."

That sent a shiver down my spine. He wasn't suggesting that there was a faction of people, or segment of society, that shouldn't vote. He was pointing the finger at all of us.

All of us in our comfy "What's the point? My vote won't make a difference" existence. Well, most of us anyway.

He was absolutely right. Trump was elected and did a bunch of, you know, highly entertaining things...provided they didn't actually have an effect on real people's lives.

This basic responsibility that comes with living in a democratic society has been decaying. People have lost faith in the "system" and the idea that their vote counts.

Of course, this is exactly what ne'er-do-wells want. They love this kind of thing.

And by "this kind of thing," I mean stupid people.

It makes winning elections easy. Simply offer the most entertaining or fun election promises and that should do the trick...because what does it matter?!

Well, of course, it DOES eventually matter. When that time comes, it's usually too late to do anything about it...at least for four or more years. If you're lucky.

This is why I propose that only smart people should vote. How do we do that?

Easy.

You remember those contests you'd get in chip bags or candy wrappers and if you won, you'd have to solve a simple math equation before you could hand it to the teenager working behind the counter before they'd give you your free Coke or whatever? Let's do that for voting.

Because it didn't actually matter if you got the equation right. You could put in any answer.

The kid behind the counter did not care.

You'd still get your free Coke.

If you didn't bother solving the math puzzle, they'd hand it back to you and ask you to fill it out.

Yes, it was dumb and probably just adhering to some legal technicality, but it worked.

It separated those who really wanted that prize and those who were too lazy.

That's what we need to start doing with voting. To separate the truly and willfully ignorant from those who actually give a damn.

Now, I'm not proposing a math question. No. Let's be more relevant to the task at hand.

Maybe you have to sort your political choices by party correctly before your vote counts.

Maybe you have to match the correct slogan to the correct candidate before your vote counts.

Anything to weed out those who haven't been paying attention and reward those who have been paying the SLIGHTEST bit of attention.

You wouldn't need to have any detailed knowledge. Just *passing* knowledge.

For example, "that's the candidate who said babies need to be given factory jobs" or "this is the candidate who kept punching people."

Broad stroke references. Anything that can reassure us that you're not simply voting for someone because you recognize their name.[2]

We need to making voting available to everyone. But maybe it's time to get people to take it a little more seriously.

---

2 This doesn't apply to those weird elections for school board trustees or comptrollers (whatever they are). Essentially, if they don't get to make laws or get the keys to government buildings, just go with your gut.

HOW TO ENTER THE UNITED STATES

SURVIVAL TIP: IT DOESN'T MATTER HOW GOOD YOUR JOKES ARE, US BORDER GUARDS WILL NOT LAUGH.

It was quite early in the morning as we approached the Canada-US border on our way to Washington, DC, for a social media convention. Maybe around 5:30 a.m.

I get nervous at the US border. I don't get nervous at any other country's border.

The US border has a way of making you feel guilty regardless if you have anything to feel guilty about. I suppose this is good. The US border guards have a job to do. They are the first line of defense to keep out ne'er-do-wells, monarchists, and Canadian actors.

I understand this level of concern and accompanying security. The US has a lot of people. Those people have money. People everywhere love money. So, I get it.

There were four of us in the car. Me, Shannon, and our two sons, Owen and Gregor. I approached the border slowly, as instructed by one of the many signs instructing you to do things.

There were no cars going through this particular land border at the time. It was super quiet. I stopped at the instructed line and waited...even though the light was green to proceed and had been green when I arrived.

These land borders are quite daunting. They have concrete barriers, numerous signs, and multiple cameras. If this is just security theatre, it should be on Broadway.

A hand appeared from inside the kiosk. Palm toward me with the second, third and pinky fingers slightly curled down. It appeared, to me at least, as a friendly, "Hey, I acknowledge you...please proceed to my kiosk and I will welcome you into my country."

It was not.

I stopped at the kiosk and the border guard immediately repeated his hand gesture.

I can't remember if he actually did have a southern drawl as he spoke, but in my mind he totally did.

"What does this mean in y'all's country?" He motioned toward his hand.

I had, in my nervousness about crossing the US border, prepared myself for a number of questions but nothing about charades or ASL.

"Hello!?" I suggested with my friendliest Canadian face.

I was wrong. Well, I wasn't wrong. In Canada it does mean that as far as I know, but it's not what that US border guard meant. He meant stop.

He quickly established that this carload of Canadians did not pose a threat and were not looking to start a new life in the United States, and he let us pass.

I breathed a sigh of relief, and we continued our journey to the US capital.

As someone who isn't American, I truly do understand why they want to make sure the borders are secure. America has many wonderful things, places, and people. Like Ryan Reynolds' movies, Ryan Reynolds' movie locations, and Ryan Reynolds. You can't just go leaving that unsecured.

However, as someone who isn't American, I find it funny when they quiz me on when I'll be leaving the US. Like everyone wants to live in America.

Of course, I know there are many people who DO wish to live in America, but I think America may be overestimating that desire for most. Especially for us in Canada.

Again, America is fantastic in lots of ways and is a magical place full of fun, amazing sights, thrilling adventures, and more...but so is Disney World.

I do not wish to live in Disney World.

Technically you can't live in Disney World, but I'm sure they'd let you stay at the resort for as long as your credit card withheld the fiscal weight.

Like with America, I realize there are some people who do wish to live there. But from my Canadian Perspective, those people are also slightly crazy.

Disney World is amazing. It is a beloved destination for many worldwide. Five days doesn't seem like enough time to fully enjoy it all, but six days seems like far too many.

The thought of wandering Main Street, USA for the rest of my life seems like a punishment.

To their credit, the security staff you meet when you enter Disney World seem to know this. Not once on my many trips to Disney World has the octogenarian Disney border guard ever drilled me on when I'm going to leave the park, what my plans were, how much money did I have access to, or whether I had any fruit—like oranges—to declare.

They are literally securing entry to THE HAPPIEST PLACE ON EARTH, and they KNOW that I will happily board that monorail eventually.

Obviously, there are massive differences between a country like the US and a theme park. I understand that.

For example, Disney World will provide basic healthcare for free. That's right. If you get sick in Disney World, they'll offer you some free basic healthcare from an actual healthcare professional to get you back on your feet and having fun.[3]

And you're not allowed to carry a gun in Disney World. About thirty people a year (staggeringly low numbers considering the number of visitors) are arrested for carrying firearms into the park.[4]

And I guess public transport is free too. Well, covered by your admission…which is kinda like a tax, I guess. Bus, boat, and monorail.

It's actually starting to sound pretty good…but no.

Even with all that and a churro, I don't want to live there.

I want to visit there, spend money, have fun, and appreciate it best as a memory.

Just like America.

---

3 Ted Wioncek III, "What To Do If You Get Sick at Walt Disney World," Touringplans.com, May 1, 2023. https://touringplans.com/blog/what-to-do-if-you-get-sick-at-walt-disney-world/

4 Dirk Libbey, "New Report Details How Many Guests Were Arrested Over Guns At Disney World Last Year," Cinemablend, March 9, 2022. https://www.cinemablend.com/movies/new-report-details-how-many-guests-were-arrested-over-guns-at-disney-world-last-year

Secrets Canadians Keep

CANADIANS ARE NOT AMERICANS

SURVIVAL TIP: WHEN MEETING SOMEONE AND YOU ARE UNSURE IF THEY ARE FROM CANADA OR THE UNITED STATES OF AMERICA, ASSUME THEY ARE FROM CANADA. CANADIANS WILL APPRECIATE THIS, AND AMERICANS WILL BE SLIGHTLY OFFENDED (WHICH NEARBY CANADIANS WILL APPRECIATE).

Pierre Trudeau, our former prime minister and our current prime minister's father...I guess that makes him our grandpa prime minister...once famously said, "There's no such thing as a model or ideal Canadian" and "We should not even be able to agree upon the kind of Canadian to choose as a model, let alone persuade most people to emulate it."

I agree. The United States is a melting pot. Canada is a mosaic in its most poetic description and a variety pack of Timbits in its most laymen's terms.

Though there are many in Canada and elsewhere who complain and attempt to mock that Canada has no identity... apart from it being "Not America."

I mostly agree with this assessment.

However, I'm also absolutely fine with it.

Let's get one thing straight: the United States of America has many lovely qualities, people, weather and, increasingly, craft beers.

Let's also be honest though, the United States of America is also entertainingly, annoyingly, and dangerously bonkers.

Don't deny it. We get American news up here in the Great White North. We see it. Every day.

Americans are largely crazy. At least according to the news, social media, and tourists.

And yes, yes...#NotAllAmericans.

But you get what I mean.

Canadians love America, but we love it in the same way we love that family member who's a little bit older and can't seem to get their shit together. I mean, we care about them, we even look up to them occasionally, but we don't want to be them.

If the "Canadian Identity" is simply being "Not American," I'm cool with that.

It may initially sound like an attempt to describe something using a negative, but it really isn't, and even if it is, we do that all the time. It's a completely valid way to describe something.

Let me explain...

If you order an Uber and two cars show up, but one is on fire, you would most likely choose the one that is not on fire. You'd probably even describe it that way. "I would like to choose the Uber that is not on fire."

If you're at a restaurant and they only offer two kinds of meals, one that's moldy and rotten and one that isn't, you would likely choose the meal that isn't moldy and rotten.

This isn't to suggest that America is on fire, moldy, and rotten.

I mean, parts of it are, but if you're American please don't take offense, those are just the parts that stand out the most and the ones we see on American news.

So, what does it mean then to say Canadians are not Americans and Canada is not America?

The obvious distinctions show up quickly…

A lot of Canadians like guns, but we don't LIKE like guns.

We just don't feel the connection to guns that some Americans do. They're not an integral part of our identity. In fact, we even celebrate that fact in one of Canada's *Heritage Minutes* TV spots.

Canada's *Heritage Minutes* TV spots were sixty second scripted vignettes that would dramatize a piece of Canadian history. Yes, that does sound kinda weird, but they are loved, and disparaging them will get you punched in the nose by any self-respecting Canuck from coast to coast to coast.

One specific episode told the story of Superintendent Sam Steele of the Northwest Mounted Police (a precursor to the Royal Canadian Mounted Police) and how he dealt with an American who was passing through Canada to pan for gold in the Yukon. He had been stopped because he was carrying gambling gear and holstered pistols—both illegal in Canada at the time. When the American tells Sam "Canada be damned," draws his pistols, and says, "I'm an American! You can't do this to me," old Sam stays true to his surname and sits there and calmly informs the American that he's getting the boot back to the USA. It finishes with the American being escorted on horseback by police officers exclaiming, "He never drew no gun!"

That's the whole point of the video...NOT being American. I love it.

The other obvious distinction is our universal healthcare system and how it differs from the USA's health insurance system.

The most basic way I can think of to describe the Canadian healthcare system is that I've never once thought about how much any medical visit or procedure has cost. From doctor's visits to the birth of my children to full surgeries. Not once. Never even occurred to me.

I present my health card and I'm good to go.

Though, to be clear, our universal healthcare system is deeply in need of help in the form of more doctors and nurses and better management. But you can still talk to any Canadian and they'll tell the tale of their cousin in America who had to sell their home after an appendectomy and don't even talk about how much it cost to have their baby two years ago.... "At least we're not in America!"

There are many more distinctions, but this book isn't about that kind of deep dive.

If you thought it was, I apologize, and also you are very bad at choosing books. You shouldn't choose something just because Ryan Reynolds' name is on the front of it. Of course, there are always attempts at drawing a circle around various things that are uniquely "Canadian," like being polite, being nice, and liking Tim Hortons.

Let me assure you, we're not all any of those things.

But at least we're not American, eh?

WHY CANADIANS ARE SO NICE

SURVIVAL TIP: NEVER QUESTION A CANADIAN'S NICENESS. ACCEPT IT AT FACE VALUE OR AS WE SAY IN CANADA "TOQUE TOTAL."

Canadians are famously polite.

We're notoriously nice to each other (generally) and to foreigners. We're so renowned for being generally good people that for decades, US travelers would sew Canadian flag patches on their backpacks when they went traveling so people would be nicer to them. That's some solid politeness branding.

Of course, we're also famous for apologizing. I recently did a video where I presented "sorry" as Canada's equivalent to Hawaii's "Aloha," in that it can be used as a greeting or a farewell. E.g., "Sorry! How are ya?" or "I gotta go! Sorry!"

Being Canadian, of course, extra points are given whether or not you pronounce "sorry" correctly as "Soary" or the American "Sahry."

I once worked with a teacher named Al Booker who would tell his students, "It's nice to be nice."

Being nice IS nice, but why are Canadians *so* nice? What is the reasoning behind their incessant cheeriness? What is at the core of their infuriating pleasant manner?

The answer is…winter.

It gets cold in Canada. Not everywhere in Canada (I need to address that quickly or people in Vancouver will lay down their car fog squeegees and brush the January cherry blossoms from their shoulders and get all irate.… Well, as irate as west coasters can get, which is the equivalent to "happy Québécois"), obviously.

Though Canadians pride themselves on surviving cold winters, winters can take their toll. Dark days, icy sidewalks, unplowed roads, frigid temperatures…it can all add up and be almost too much to bear. So, we fake being happy.

Well, "fake" is a strong word. Let's say we try really, REALLY hard to be happy. We do this because every Canadian during winter is one wet sock away from snapping. We know that under that balaclava there may be smiling eyes, but thoughts of homicide might not be far behind.

Our national politeness has been ingrained in us over generations of harsh winters as a survival skill. It keeps Canadians from turning on other Canadians, but it also aids in our countrywide delusions of being okay with winter. If we act happy about winter we might, just might, forget about how nature is trying to kill us.

This forced niceness has us saying things like "at least it's a dry cold," "I heard it's going above zero next week!" or "I don't mind the cold!" All lies we tell ourselves so that we can pretend we're okay with 1/4 to 2/3 of our year being dominated by weather that actively wants us dead.

We also maintain this ruse so that people who don't live in Canada don't think we're insane for living in Canada. The thinking being that, if we seem nice and polite, maybe winters aren't that bad, and gosh, they almost look fun.

Lies. All lies. The whole country has been lying to you.

I may be overstating this, but I don't think I am.

To better understand Canadian niceness, imagine it as a fuel. A fuel you burn to keep warm. Feeling a little chilly? Compliment someone. Cold wind starting to nip at your ears? Try being amenable to something you have no interest in doing.

Canadian politeness and niceness are a means to an end, and that end is Spring. Not like early spring either, when the roads are sloshy pits of brown but real spring...like mid-June.

So should you find yourself in the company of a Canadian and you are marveling at their politeness, know that it masks a toque thin grasp on sanity. But enjoy it and receive it at face-value. Much like sleepwalkers, it is dangerous to awaken Canadians from their polite trance-like state, so don't risk questioning it.

Will this ever change? Well, like every other thing in our lives, climate change is a major issue and threatens not only the planet but also specifically Canadian politeness. As we all have agreed (at least the less dumb ones of us), climate change is the root cause of extreme weather. This aspect of climate change will not be an issue for Canadians, as most of our weather is extreme already. However, climate change will also bring rising temperatures, and that means milder winters... which means Canadians, in between devastating floods, forest fires, and tornadoes, might not be as cold during winter. Which in turn means that Canadians may lose their need to be polite and we may live to see the day when Canadians are no longer nice.

Even more concerning, it's already started. Just look at Ted Cruz, Kevin O'Leary, and Jordan Peterson.

Will climate change leave nothing unscathed??

But rest easy. Canadian politeness is resilient. It can take a few hits and it won't only turn the other cheek, it will complement the strength of the blow and suggest they try again.

Canadian niceness isn't going away anytime soon.

Sorry.

CANADIAN CUISINE IS AN ACT OF DEFIANCE

SURVIVAL TIP: WHEN VISITING CANADA OR A CANADIAN, BRACE YOURSELF PHYSICALLY AND EMOTIONALLY DURING MEALS OR SNACKS.

I love butter tarts.

This is no secret. I have exclaimed my love for them countless times online. I famously (no, honestly…65 million+ people have watched the video) conjured up a metaphorical definition for them in a video back in 2017 where I said that "if you put sex and gold into a blender, you'd get a butter tart." I stand by that. So much so that I named my own line of booze S&G because it has a hint of butter tart (it's not sweet or a liqueur, it's more like a bourbon).

However, that all said, the actual ingredients of a butter tart are unholy. They are as follows…sugar, butter, corn syrup, egg, salt, and vanilla extract. And that's just the filling. The pastry shell has even more sugar. They are sin in three bites.

But let's be honest. They're also terrifically bad for you. There is no "Butter Tart Diet."

Fellow Canadian Mike Myers once said that all Scottish cuisine is built on a dare. As a child to Scottish immigrants, I agree with him, but I think we can then proclaim the following:

Canadian cuisine is an act of defiance.

Think about it. Starting with the butter tart. A sugary sweet tart type treat that is nothing but a thinly veiled excuse to eat a fistful of sugar and butter.

We Canadians look to the gods of weather, interminably long car rides between cities, good health and dental care, and say, "FIE! We will eat what might kill us or give us cavities to stay alive!"

Canadian cuisine is an act of defiance.

Let's talk about poutine.

What's not really great for you? French fries.

What's not super healthy to eat too much of? Cheese curds.

What's universally regarded as a liquid heart attack? Gravy.

Stack 'em up, eh. We're going to Poutine Town!

Poutine is arguably not good for you. Actually, no. Scratch that. It's universally established that it's not good for you, but we here in Canada have made it our national dish. The dish we present to the world and say, "Here is Canada on a plate… or paper take-out box. Eat it and die."

It doesn't end there. Taking a leaf from our Scottish ancestors and their haggis, someone in Quebec at some point said, "You think I'm going to throw these random animal parts out? We'll see about that. I'm going to bake them into a pie," and tourtière was born.

Even maple syrup has a defiant origin. Faced with the possibility of freezing to death in the frozen north, we decided to start sucking trees and telling people how great it is (and it is).

Pure defiance. Pure defiance to nature and life in general. An edible middle finger. It's a side of Canada that many outside people rarely notice.

Faced with the constant struggles of trying to stay alive during bitterly cold winters, not enough Canadian NHL teams, wannabe American-style politicians, the absence of Zellers (the predecessor to Target in Canada), and the short but entirely predictable demise of all 133 Target Canada stores because they forgot we're not America, Canadians are angry, but their niceness prevents them from lashing out. So, we create foods that we eat in defiance.

Don't believe me? Who do you think invented pineapple on pizza. That's right. Canada. "Hawaiian" Pizza was invented by Sam Panopoulos in Chatham, Ontario. We don't know his reasons for sure, but it was probably just to piss people off... and it's delicious.

Ginger Beef? That's right, the candied and deep-fried strips of beef that taste like dying but in a good way? Invented in Calgary, Alberta, by George Wong at the Silver Inn.

Don't even get me started on Jellied Moose Nose, Maple Slaw, or Oreilles de Crisse. Not to mention Indigenous (to whom we owe a lot here in Canada) specialties like Muktuk, which is just whale skin and blubber.

All of these were created, I believe, as an act of defiance. A resounding "fuck you" to propriety, expectation, and caution. An unwavering wink and a smile to life that says, "let's fucking go."

Living in a cold and vast northern country requires resilience. Short days and long nights in winter. A small population in an expansive land. It requires a sense of humor and will to survive and thrive. And sometimes that requires looking adversity straight in the eye and saying, "Want a butter tart?"

LET ME DEBUNK A CANADIAN MYTH (OR TWO)

SURVIVAL TIP: MANY CANADIANS WILL TELL YOU THAT ALL CANADIANS LIKE WINTER—THEY ARE LYING.

What I'm about to reveal to you is so incendiary and such a betrayal to my homeland that I may not be able to show my face in a Canadian Tire for a week.

There's a lot here, so let's start slowly but with a biggie:

Not all Canadians love winter.

It's true. Some of us hate it but put up with it because it really cuts down on crime. That's true. Not that surprising when you think about it though. You know hard it would be to break into a house in Sudbury and steal things in January? The police could literally track you down by following your footprints in the snow.

Winter is nature's way of killing things. You know how they get rid of bedbugs by cranking up the heat and then they die? Same idea except the temperature drops and we're nature's bedbugs.

People who aren't from Canada think winter is like living in a snow globe. This is accurate…for about a day. Then that heavenly fluff that fell from the sky turns into a brown gritty slush that doesn't go away until mid-March, if we're lucky. It becomes a road-covering salty brine that reminds us that winter may go away but it will always come back…and it may be coming for you.

Here's another one:

Not all Canadians love hockey.

It's true. Even I only kinda like hockey. I mean, it's a great fast game but also involves a lot of spitting. Outside of bare-knuckle boxing and scrabble with my wife's grandmother, it's also the only sport that actively encourages fist fights….but even then, doesn't award points to the victor.

Growing up in Canada, participation in hockey, in some form, is expected of us. When my parents immigrated to Canada from Scotland in 1968, they were eager to fit in to the local culture of a small town, which meant renting horses (that's true, but let's save that story) and playing hockey. My dad joined the work sponge-puck league with some friends and played every week. My mom attended the top league team in our city's games on a Friday. Which coincidentally were played in the same arena where Wayne Gretzky scored his first goal in an official hockey game when he was six years old in 1967. As Canadians, we are required by law to know that.

They even put me, their little cherubic translucent-skinned angel, into hockey as soon as I could skate. Which was about two weeks out of the womb. The league for kids under ten was called "Brownies." No, I do not know why. You started, as I did, in Brownie C, then moved to Brownie B, then Brownie A, then did a second year in Brownie A where you suddenly didn't recognize anyone on your team and all your friends seemed to be playing in the next level Junior league.... That second year of Brownie A may have been specific to me. Though it should be noted that I scored four goals even though I was on defense (to be fair most of the kids were quite smaller than me that second year around). I gave up after year two of Brownie A because a lot of the guys weren't getting ready into their hockey gear at home anymore. They'd change in the locker room. I vividly remember one Saturday morning as I sat in my full hockey gear, and skates with skate guards on, watching *Captain Caveman*, eating Alpha-Bits cereal, and my dad saying it was time to go, and me replying, "I think I'm done." He concurred.

Even after all that, I still like hockey, but I certainly don't love it. I'm certainly not the only Canadian who feels that way. I'd rather stay home, watch *Captain Caveman*, and eat my bowl of Alpha-Bits.

Which brings me to food and drink.

I won't touch on poutine here, because of a couple of reasons. One, it's delicious even though it's a heart attack in a takeaway container, and two, I don't need the Quebeckers' wrath (*Pardonne-moi. La poutine est la nourriture des dieux*). (For more on poutine, see previous chapter.)

However, I will debunk one more Canadian myth:

We don't all love Tim Hortons.

Let me be clear. There is nothing wrong with Tim Hortons. They make fine, though diminishing in size recently, donuts. They brew fine coffee. Nothing wrong with it, but we Canadians don't all *love* it. The reason it seems like we love it is because Tim Hortons stores are EVERYWHERE. I live in a town of 32,000 people and there are three. There were four, but two of them were within one hundred yards of each other, and that just seemed too silly. The ubiquity of Tim Hortons might make it seem like every Canadian loves Tim Hortons, but in reality, it's just there.

It's always there.

I will add an important note to finish this off:

Should you NOT be a Canadian and meet a Canadian in the USA, UK, Europe, or anywhere on the planet else except Canada…we will defend winter, hockey, and Tim Hortons to the death.

Sorry.

THEY'RE CANADIAN, YOU KNOW

SURVIVAL TIP: IF EVER ASKED WHERE SOME TRUSTED AND RESPECTED CELEBRITY IS FROM, THE ANSWER IS CANADA.

We do it all the time.

Every damn time.

Watching a TV show, a movie, the news, something online, doesn't matter. We Canadians seemingly gain life force from it. Four words that roll forth out of our poutine-greased lips with ease…

They're Canadian, you know.

Canada, in its ultimate Canadian-ness, has a hard time celebrating and elevating our own while they're here in Canada. Of course, there are exceptions like Rick Mercer, The Tragically Hip, Mark Critch, etc., but those celebrities feel like our own private celebrities. Like the difference between a family room and a living room. One is just for you and you can enjoy it with low maintenance, the other is only for special occasions like when America visits and you're not allowed to sit in there otherwise.

The Canadian celebrities that are the "living rooms" are people like Ryan Reynolds (thank you again for the touching and heartfelt foreword, Ryan), Colin Mochrie (for the last time, stop calling me Drew), The Property Bothers (the funny one AND the good looking one), and Michael J. Fox (I have no joke for Michael, he's just cool). The list goes on and on…but no need to memorize it. If there is a Canadian in the room while you're watching something with a Canadian in it, the Canadian in the room will tell you that the person you're watching is Canadian. They'll present it as an aside but it's really all they want to talk about.

If allowed, they will continue the conversation with interesting and important (to them) facts about the Canadian you're currently watching. Where they went to school, where they grew up, where they used to work, and in the case of Avril Lavigne, the Home Hardware in Napanee that you pass on the 401 who sponsored the kids' soccer team that Avril played on when she was a kid, and she wore the same t-shirt on her first *Saturday Night Live* appearance.

Just recently, I mentioned to my sons that Keanu Reeves went to high school just down the street from their apartment in Toronto. This information will serve them well in life during future viewings of the *Bill and Ted's Excellent Adventure* franchise. I'm a good father.

There is something a little perverse about it, and by perverse, I mean completely regular Canadian behavior. Why are we so enamored by the Canadians who leave? Do they need to find success elsewhere before we validate them as worthy? In some ways, yes.

However, I think there's more to it than that. I think it's about showing our worth to the world. It's about realizing that even though we're in this sparsely populated country, we can still have an impact on the world.

It's also about getting one over on our American friends.

Actually, that may be most of it. Maybe all of it.

Forget the other stuff I said about worth and impact. It's all about telling our American friends "Ha! Those famous people you love and trust? All Canucks!" From movie stars to musicians, and newscasters to comedians, Canada dominates. And we LOVE that.

You see, living in Canada, we are under a constant tidal wave of American culture. American media reaches across our border and hooks us in. Our television networks show American sitcoms; our game shows are just American gameshows with "Canada" stuck at the end of their name. Sometimes it gets a bit much. So, when one of our own sneaks into American media and shows up on our TV screens, it feels like a win. Like we've played the system.

Not much gave us greater joy than when CNN hired Daniel Dale as a fact checker. Most of us in Canada almost passed out from forgetting to breathe in an effort to be the first to let Americans know that Daniel is from Toronto (well, Thornhill...but close enough). Sure, there are a myriad of other prominent Canadians in American news like Ali Velshi, Kim Brunhuber, Keith Morrison, Morley Safer, Peter Jennings, and more, but none were in positions as delicious as "fact checker." This was momentous. It was like having your older sibling come to you for help sorting their life out. The same older sibling that would continuously tease you and mock you for being so much smaller was now coming to you for advice on how to get out of a bad relationship. It was a special time for Canada.

Lest this sound antagonistic, it is not. Canada loves American Culture—well, not all of it, but a lot of it, because it's so enjoyable or engaging and usually really good. It's like living above a live theatre production version of a blockbuster action/comedy/horror movie. Knowing some of us Canadians are part of what make it so enticing, is pretty great, eh.

Family Are the Other People on the Plane Before It Crash Landed in the Jungle

FAMILY ARE THE OTHER PEOPLE ON THE PLANE

SURVIVAL TIP: AS YOUR FAMILY GROWS AND EXTENDS TO INCLUDE NEW RELATIONSHIPS, ENCOURAGE USEFUL NEWCOMERS LIKE MECHANICS OR HAIRDRESSERS.

I loved the show *Lost*.

Well, I loved it right up until the last episode, then I hated it. And yes, yes, I know there are those of you out there that say the negative reaction by all reasonable people to the finale of that show was unwarranted and argue that it all makes sense. Those of you are wrong.

It sucked.

However, one of the things that I've often thought about was how when they crash landed on that island, they had to quickly establish who had what skills that would increase their chances of survival.

I don't have a fear of flying. My view is that once you're up in the air, there's precious little you can do about it...plus you could die getting up from the toilet. So, stop worrying and enjoy the flight. You're in a machine that works IN THE SKY. That's pretty cool.

Anyway, since *Lost*, whenever I'm on a plane, I take a look at my other passengers and try to determine their worth should we need to crash land. Who will gather or hunt for food? Who will make the food? Who will protect us from wild animals or "Others?" Who will make sure we have shelter?

But then my mind wanders further to the really important stuff: Who will cut my hair?

Of course, all I have to go on is outward appearance, maybe what they're reading or watching, and what they pull out of their carry-on. I don't have much time to get to know them, so should we crash land, I guess we'll just have to hope someone knows how to cut my hair without exposing too much of my bald spot.

This is very similar to your family. Both close family and extended family. With your close family (parents, children, etc.), you don't have really any choice in who they turn out to be as people and what their marketable jungle skill will be.

However, with extended family, and I'm defining that as the people you marry, the people your close family marries or as-good-as marries, you have a little bit of influence. You can help guide them to people who may have desirable skills that will somehow improve your own life. Like an accountant, mechanic, plumber, electrician, hairdresser, or even a lawyer if you're desperate.

This window of influence is fleeting. Seeds need to be planted far in advance. You can't wait for your family members to fall in love and then find out their beloved is a social media content creator. Useless.

No, you need to lay the groundwork early. I've been doing this with a friend recently as she slowly heads out in search of a potential new partner. To be clear, I am not suggesting that I would stand in the way of love simply because I would stand to gain. Absolutely not. The heart wants what the heart wants… but if the heart wants a rich guy with a nice boat and a summer cottage I can use for free, would that really hurt anyone?

So, I've been gently dropping hints with her like, "Know any rich guys with boats?" and "It'd be great if you met a nice guy with a summer cottage I can use for free." You know, subtle little bits of guidance that might steer her toward a new love that will directly benefit me as well.

But even with a mighty effort, you don't usually get a final say on who becomes a part of your family, apart from your own spouse and it's too late to do anything about them now anyway. Just ask Shannon. You simply have to like them, at least in small doses, and hope they have valuable skills.

All this to say, your family are the other people on the plane when it crash lands in the jungle. It's luck of the draw. You get what you get. Maybe no one knows how to fashion a shelter out of palm tree leaves or turn a wild boar into a delicious pork tenderloin, and that's okay.

Because just like the plucky people on the plane in *Lost*, they worked together to make things better for each other. Sure, some turned on each other, but we've all gotten a little hot under the collar during family get-togethers. The important thing is to remember that your family members are all you've got in this jungle of life. You need to rely on them, and they need to rely on you.

And it's just a weird jungle…not a metaphor for purgatory and we've all been dead this whole time.

Maybe.

YOU'RE THE NPC IN YOUR KID'S LIFE

SURVIVAL TIP: YOU HAVE ABOUT THREE YEARS TOPS BEFORE YOUR KID IS NO LONGER A CHARACTER IN YOUR LIFE AND YOU BECOME A CHARACTER IN THEIR'S.

Having a baby is fun.

I'm not talking about making the baby. Though that is usually pretty fun as well. I'm referring to that magical time when you leave the hospital (if you chose a hospital to have the baby in) with this little living creature in a car seat and head home to submerge yourself into full-time baby time.

I remember that feeling from both of our sons. It was so exciting. Like when you'd buy a budgie at the pet store at the mall and they'd stick it in a special small pet take out box and you'd be excited all of the way home so you can introduce it to its new life, except that with babies they might ACTUALLY learn to talk someday. Useless budgerigars.

When your kids are just babies, they're really just accessories to you. Like one of the women who cart around tiny dogs in their purse. It's helps define them. The tiny dog is incidental. That may sound harsh, but think about it. You get to dress them how you want. You get to name them. You get to cart them around in little carriers and they suddenly change who you are and how people see you. You can even take them to restaurants or shopping. Babies, initially, are like acid wash jeans. They're something you have that affects how the world perceives you.

I'm not saying babies are unimportant. Absolutely not. I'm also not saying taking care of babies is a breeze. Not in the slightest. Being a parent has been the hardest job I've ever had…and I've worked in a record store where people would ask for "that song that has the word 'love' in it." I know hard work.

However, when they're little babies, your kids are just part of your belongings. Like an item you collect in a video where you're the main character.

Then something changes. It changes rapidly. It happens around the time your babies become autonomous. Not just walking but walking to something that caught their interest so they *need* to investigate it further. Or in the case of our eldest child, Owen, who was three at the time, we were having a meal at the pub sitting with our backs to the restaurant while he faced out when the server walked by and said, "Hi, Owen," and he waved back nonchalantly.

It was staggering for myself and my wife. The server didn't acknowledge us. She didn't come over and say hi to us, and then turn to Owen and say, "Howz widdle Owen!" and we didn't tell Owen to wave.

He had had a social interaction that was entirely independent from us, his parents. It was slightly terrifying.

In that moment it dawned on me. He was no longer a character in our lives, we were characters in his.

I had gone from the main character in my story to a Non-Playable Character (NPC) in his.

Of course, I would still be living my own story, but I was no longer just "me with a baby," I was "me who happens to have a kid."

It was difficult at first. Actually, it was really difficult for a long time. As a parent, you try to balance giving your kids some freedom and autonomy with that pesky thing of wanting to keep them alive.

The same process happened with our youngest, Gregor, though it wasn't at the pub. It was seeing him interacting with other kids on a school field trip. Talking to his classmates and teachers as if he had his own feelings, thoughts, and views. You know, like a real person.

It's very strange but it also, I think, helps make you a better parent. Not that I'm a great parent...*waits for someone to tell me I am*...oh, right, this is a book and fishing for compliments doesn't work.

Being an NPC in your kid's life takes a little bit of the pressure off. You don't have to worry about your fashion sense being judged by others because it doesn't matter, you're not the star of this story. Your kid is. You don't have worry about trying to be cool because you probably aren't, and it doesn't matter. Your only role is to help propel the story of your kid's adventures.

You can still have your own quests and those quests will one day make you the main character again in your own story (when your kids no longer need you as a constant NPC), but in the meantime you get to enjoy being a supporting character ready to provide some weird dialogue and advice when your kid's main character decides to interact with you.

It's a good gig.

BEFORE YOU'RE IN THE SANDWICH

SURVIVAL TIP: BE AWARE IF YOU WILL BE IN THE SANDWICH BEFORE YOU'RE IN THE SANDWICH.

My dad was a bit irate.

I was calling from the UK. I would call once a week to check in. This was not because I'm a bad son but rather because it was the mid-'90s and texting, video calls, social media, and free VOIP calling hadn't been invented yet.

Yes, I'm that old.

My dad was irate. Not super irate, just a bit. You see, I had been living in the UK for about a year with Shannon while she went to teacher's college, and I worked at Virgin. In my crafty obliviousness as an excellently immature twenty-five-year-old, I had not had any of my charge card bills sent to my new address and simply expected my mom and dad to take care of them for me. I don't even remember pausing about that decision.

Anyway, my dad was upset because he wanted to know what I had purchased at the local gas station in Helensburgh where we lived at the time. He asked what I could possibly have spent $75 Canadian on at an Esso station (gas was much cheaper in those days and we drove a Fiat Uno). I wracked my brain and then remembered that we had put the equivalent of about $15 gas in the car in order to get us to a friend's house in nearby Glasgow. It didn't feel right arriving for a mid-afternoon visit empty handed so I bought a dozen donuts at the Esso station's convenient Dunkin' Donuts Express counter at the same time as paying for the gas. I handed over my American Express card, signed the slip, and then headed out the door.

It turns out American-style donuts at a gas station in the middle of Scotland are quite expensive. Around $5 Canadian each. I had bought twelve. So, I had spent $60 on donuts alone and the bill for the donuts and gas had now reached my dad... who had to pay it.

I didn't even check the price of the donuts when I bought them. I would never see the bill so what was the worry?

This year, my two sons, Owen and Gregor, did some audio and video work with Jonathan Scott (yes, of the *Property Brothers*) at his and Zooey Deschanel's new home. I had secured an American Express card for each of them for the project, so that while they were gathering footage in California they could handle hotels, Ubers, food, and gear costs.

However, I know their father. He is me. So, I made sure there was a budget available from the project that would cover the incoming expenses. Full disclosure, both Owen and Gregor are a million times more responsible than I was at their age...but again, I know their father.

There's a brief period of adulthood for most where you are only responsible for yourself and your own interests. This time exists before having children and before your parents turn into really old children. It's referred to as the Sandwich Generation. Coined by Dorothy Miller and Elaine Brody back in 1981, the term refers to those middle-aged persons who take care of their own children and their aging parents. You know, they're in between, like a sandwich.

Here's the thing...you gotta know you're going to be in the sandwich before you're in the sandwich. Then you can properly enjoy that time.

Like everything good in life, it's easier said than done though. Life before you're in the sandwich can be colossally shit. Sure, as a kid, you can sail obliviously through life, but when you get to your early twenties, the seas start to get rough. That sociobiological pressure of trying to figure out who you are and where you fit in with society takes over. Everyone that age becomes like squirrels when the weather starts to get cold. Lots of frantic scrambling and preparation for the unknown ahead. Which is the awful part. You're furiously preparing for the complete unknown.

But here's the good news. It generally always works out. Or more to the point, it doesn't matter how well prepared you are, life thinks your plans are hilarious. It will always throw you unexpected challenges.

So, try not to worry too much. Worry a little. That helps you get the basics in order but apart from that, just know that the only thing you can know is that someday you're going to be in the sandwich. Do your best to enjoy your time not in the sandwich.

Life in the sandwich isn't awful but it's certainly not as carefree.

This time before you're in the sandwich is fleeting. Enjoy it.

THE GOLDEN BOY

SURVIVAL TIP: THOSE WHO CAN DO NO WRONG DO AS MUCH WRONG AS THE REST OF US; THEY JUST SMILE MORE.

The back room just off the kitchen was packed with dry goods.

It was organized like a tiny grocery store. Pasta, cans of soup, jars of sauce, rice, sugar, flour, bathroom tissue, paper towels, you name it, if it was a non-perishable item, it was there. My grandmother would buy things in bulk when they went on sale and then offer them up to myself and my wife to take as we needed. I guess it was like our own personal food bank except it was presented to us more as our own private bodega.

My gran had put in shelves to keep things organized. It was very impressive. It was even—weirdly—retailed superbly. All labels facing out, stock brought forward on the shelf, featured items by the door. It was amazing that my gran had done all this for me, her "Golden Boy," as she'd call me.

Except it turned out it wasn't my gran that had done all this on her own. My sister had been the one summoned to give our gran a ride to the actual grocery store when stock was running low, or some item went on sale. It was my sister who carried the groceries to the car and out of the car. It was my sister who did the superb job of retailing every item and kept me aware that there was a great deal on free-to-me Kraft Mac & Cheese (Kraft Dinner to Canadians) that week.

I only found that out about a year ago. My sister was fine with it, thankfully. It made me feel a little weird about the whole "Golden Boy" title. To be clear, my gran would refer to my sister, Debbie (yes, yes, Debbie Reynolds...but not Princess Leia's mom and that's not even her name anymore) as her "Golden Girl." The show *The Golden Girls* came into being after she gave her that nickname...I think. Also, myself and my sister were my gran's only grandchildren. We didn't have a third sibling that my gran relegated to "Bronze Boy" or "Silver Girl" or anything like that. My gran wasn't a monster. Both my sister and I were "Golden," it's just that one of us was the kind of "Golden" that restocked shelves in a pretend grocery store for the sole benefit of the other "Golden."

It was good being the "Golden Boy." It had steeled my resolve and boosted my confidence many times in my life. For the most part, it felt good, but this revelation about my sister had left me feeling a little guilty and more than a little introspective.

I'm fairly vain and usually feel I deserve more than I merit, so the guilt faded quickly.

The introspection went on a bit longer but here's what I determined...

Sometimes privilege is thrust upon you. You don't have a choice. You just got lucky and that's not because you necessarily deserved it or earned it. It just is.

You can't control that, but you CAN control what you do with that privilege.

It's good to pump up our kids' confidence. It's good to let them know that they have a solid foundation beneath that is pushing them upwards and ready to catch them if they stumble...but we also fully believe they won't stumble, because they're awesome. Kids need us as cheerleaders. Kids need us to make them feel special because they are.

I'm not referring to giving them false hope. My gran never told me I was great at hockey despite welcoming me into her home right across the street from the arena for hot chocolate after every hockey game. She never told me I was good with money when I was continually asking to borrow some. But the things I was kinda good at or was passionate about, she would support me and boost my confidence.

That kind of thing is really good for kids. Life is hard enough. Everybody needs fans.

The important part is once your kids know they're special, you need to encourage them to make others feel special too. They need to become someone else's cheerleader. Not all the time but sometimes. They need to learn that the things that happen for them may not be happening for everyone, but because they're special, they can help change that.

I'm not purporting to say that I, as the "Golden Boy," have special magical powers (apart from my congenial nature, cuteness, and charisma that basically leaps off the page), but I am saying that I'm aware that the reason I felt/feel special is because of the efforts of others.

So, it's Golden Boy's turn to make others feel golden too.

FAMILY IS NOT WORTH IMPRESSING

SURVIVAL TIP: NEVER WORRY ABOUT WHAT YOUR FAMILY THINKS OF YOU, THEY ARE LEGALLY BOUND TO YOU.

I rarely see my wife's family.

This isn't by design but rather geography.

Which perhaps is by design.

We live about six hours away from the majority of them and only occasionally see them at the shared family cottage.

Those visits used to last for a few days, but as everyone has aged, those visits normally only last an afternoon, a dinner, and a chat afterwards, before people climb back into their cars and head for home.

This is a mutual arrangement. As was confirmed on a recent trip to the cottage when one of my wife's uncles said he liked these short visits because, though he loved spending time with family, he—

"—wanted to keep loving them?" I offered.

"Exactly," he replied, relieved. Punctuating his victorious attempt to avoid being the one who said such a thing with a finger-gun click.

This was a huge relief for me, as I used to fret constantly about failing to impress Shannon's family.

When Shannon and I had started going out and I met her family, I was working retail…but I was convinced that I was a rock star in-waiting. I had been writing and recording music since I was in my early teens and really felt that the universe would note how much time and effort I had put in and would reward me any day now. I grappled with how to convince others that my musical ambition was legitimate (it absolutely was) and merited (uh, a little less so). I needed to be taken seriously by them and I wanted them to realize just how lucky Shannon was to have hitched her wagon to my rock 'n' roll rocket ship.

What a waste of time and worry. I didn't need to impress them, but I felt compelled to.

I was worried that if they weren't impressed by me, they might have a word with Shannon and convince her she should ditch me. Had I completely forgotten every lesson learned from watching teen movies and that this attempt at derision would merely secure her love of me while we danced to OMD's "If You Leave" at the prom?

However, I'd repeatedly show up with CDs of my latest creation. I'd drop stories of how fifteen seconds of a song I recorded had been used in a television show somewhere in Eastern Europe I think but we wouldn't get that show here anyway so don't bother checking. How stupid. I wince when I remember back to those days. (Even though we have this thing called the Internet and can now confirm if fifteen seconds of my song was on Eastern European TV, don't go searching it. All those tapes were erased.)

Do you really even want family to be impressed by you? I mean, it sounds nice to be admired, but it also sounds kind of exhausting. Never letting your guard down? Always keeping the show running? Constantly worried that one day they WON'T be impressed?

No, family is not worth impressing.

But damn it, I caught myself trying to do exactly that on our most recent visit.

I've gone from desperately wanting to be taken seriously as a musician to desperately wanting to be taken seriously as...a guy who works in comedy?

What madness!

But there I was...dropping names and places into my stories in an effort to impress people that have known me for almost thirty years and through some pretty impressive (in its most widely defined sense) haircuts.

"I was just saying that in a video meeting with these people IN LOS ANGELES."

"I remember when we were in DC...and I was INVITED TO THE WHITE HOUSE."

"I think they texted me that picture, let me scroll past this text message FROM PROPERTY BROTHER JONATHAN SCOTT."

"A great piece of advice that someone told me...who was that again, OH RIGHT, IT WAS RYAN REYNOLDS."

I almost felt dirty afterwards.

And why? There is zero need to impress these family members.

It's too late.

Shannon and I have two grown children.

We've been married for decades.

They're stuck with me.

But it not only applies for those who have years of familiarity. It applies to anyone.

Significant others need to be impressed by you. At least initially.

Potential employers need to be impressed by you. At least for as long as you want the job.

Family does not need to be impressed by you.

This does not excuse you, of course, from congeniality. It's important to be polite, easy to get along with, and to do your part.

In much the same way as a chair in a waiting room provides function but does not need to be impressive, you just need to be there when needed.

Of all the people in the world you should be trying to impress, family is not one of them.

There is no need to impress family.

Family is not worth impressing.

We should revel in that knowledge. Take our shoes off. Have another drink. Relax.

Technology Is Obsolete

SELF-CHECKOUTS ARE THE HARBINGERS OF DOOM

SURVIVAL TIP: ACQUAINT YOURSELF WITH THE CASHIERS AT YOUR LOCAL SUPERMARKET AS THEY EACH HOLD A SPECIAL SKILL AND YOU CAN CHOOSE YOUR CHECKOUT LANE WISELY.

I love self-checkouts.

I should qualify that statement. As someone with mild social anxiety and hobby-level loathing of people in general, I love the *idea* of self-checkouts. They are a way for me to reduce my interaction with other humans. No worry of the cashier judging your purchases. No need for me to nervously use my line when checking out a weird selection of items, which originated when I was in the Bahamas and was purchasing a family-sized bag of chocolate M&Ms, a large bottle of Pepto Bismol, and some bongos.... "Now THAT's a party!"

There's also an implied efficiency. It reduces your visit down to the basic transaction. I want these items. How much are these items? Here is payment for my items. No goodbyes necessary.

No muss. No fuss.

At least that's how it's supposed to go, but it doesn't. The machine wonders what this extra weight is on its scale, when it knows damn well it's the reusable shopping bag it asked me about at the beginning of the transaction. Or you have one or more items that are too large to be lifted and suspended over the useless scanner that has suddenly turned into a cat in its attempts to avoid looking where you want it to look.

Worst of all, to me at least, are the huge iPad type things at fast food restaurants. Listen, I'm all for cutting down my time spent giving my lunch order to a seriously uninterested teenager who probably only hears the word "old" whenever I open my mouth. Of course, this doesn't reflect on all teenagers who work hard at fast food restaurants. There are some great kids and out of the eight million times I've been to a fast food joint I've encountered at least four.

But the big iPad things only look like they're going to save you time and make your experience efficient and generally better. That is, until you get close enough and you can see every other person's grubby fingerprints. Then once you stumble through the jerky on-screen order process that you're pretty sure is being run on Windows Vista and is seemingly less "touch to order" and more "we'll give you something close to what you tried to touch, you wanted four Filet o'Fish, right?" you realize that the teen who was behind the counter when you came in is now graduated from university, married, and her and her toddler are waiting to use the machine after you.

Self-checkouts all suffer from the same issue. Whether they be in grocery stores, pharmacies, fast food restaurants, or wherever, they all assume that every human that uses them will know what to do and will do that in a clean and efficient manner. We will not. We are idiots. All humans are dumb.

We will hit the wrong button. We will type in the code for melons when we're buying a mango because, close enough. We will lean on the scale. We will use our car keys to tap the screen. We will remember our coupon *after* paying. We are useless.

Machines don't get that. They don't understand.

But you know who does?

Real live cashiers.

They get it. By being human as well, they recognize that we're all idiots.

Now, to be completely transparent on this issue, if given the choice in a new or unfamiliar environment, I will always choose the self-checkout. I may know that I'm an idiot, but if I don't know the cashiers, I can't tell if they're idiots as well. As the old saying goes, when one idiot meets another idiot, you don't want to be one of those idiots.

However, in my local supermarket, my wife and I have scoped out the good cashiers. This did involve some trial and error, but we feel it has paid off. We now know which cashiers are the most efficient. Which are the most helpful. Which ones excel at grocery bag Tetris. Which ones are the best coupon redeemers. Which ones are the friendliest. Which are the most likely to engage in chitchat and which are the least likely to engage in any chitchat.

Then, depending on the day we're having, what we're trying to purchase, or how busy we or the store are, we make a choice.

They're not all one age or gender either. Thinking the old lady cashiers will be the best is a rookie mistake. Sometimes the young guy is your man.

Self-checkouts can't do all that.

But if none of our favorites are working or available, we use the self-checkout…and we love it.

LANDLINES AND GOOD TIMES

SURVIVAL TIP: THE GOOD OLD DAYS ARE ONLY REMEMBERED THAT WAY BECAUSE NO ONE HAD CAMERAPHONES.

You know how some people say they grew up in the wrong era?

Well, I think I grew up in the perfect era for me.

We'll ignore the geographic, political, gender, race, and economic issues that played a massive part in my ability to achieve contentment in this time period for the sake of crafting some really nice surface-level-only nostalgia here.

I love technology. I grew up surrounded by a relentless promise of a better tomorrow thanks to technology. Computers were going to be in every home!

Unfathomable!

We'd be able to see the person we were talking to on the telephone!

Mind-blowing!

Soon those telephones would fit in our pockets, and we could take them anywhere!

Holy moly!

We'd be on the cusp of launching a spaceship that could be used again and again!

Beam me up!

It seemed like the world I would watch on the original *Star Trek* reruns was starting to happen right in front of my eyes in real life.

This is what I mean when I say I think I was born in the perfect era for me. The amazing technology that I was watching change from concepts to real tangible things had been dreamt of for decades. Those *Star Trek* reruns were from twenty years prior. Well, before I was born. Many kids would have watched them and dreamed of the day they would become reality, but I was watching WHILE they were becoming reality. My sense of wonder perfectly peaked at the exact window in time when technology was taking massive steps forward.

It's served to maintain my sense of wonder today as a rapidly aging man who still holds his smartphone in his hands like Mufasa holding Simba and launches into a monologue about how amazing it is that I have the power to connect with anyone on the planet, find the answer to practically any question you could conjure up, take a photo or video of wherever I am and whatever I'm doing (within reason), orient myself on a map and find the precise directions to anywhere else on the map, and watch videos of cats trying to jump on things but missing.

Phenomenal.

It's too easy to take the technology of today for granted, unless you compare it with the technology of yesterday. Then you wonder how people survived.

When I was my sons' ages, cellular phones were around, but only rich people had them and they only worked in big cities. I thought we were living in the future when our family got a cordless phone. You know, one of the ones with the pull-out antennae that would almost work in a different room from the base.

I grew up with one phone in our living room and one in our basement. Same number, obviously. If my mom and dad could sense things were getting a little too hot and heavy on a call with a girlfriend, they'd pick up the other extension and tell me it was time to hang up. When people wanted to call me, they had to hope I was in the building they were calling. When my wife and lived in Scotland in the mid-'90s, we only had one landline phone, and it was located in the front hall of our flat by the door and had a three-foot cord making it conveniently located for no one.

I stay in constant contact with both my parents and my kids these days via texts or video calls. When I was growing up, my parents would go for days without hearing from or seeing me. That was good and bad.

"Good" because it feels like we worried less back in the day.

"Bad" because we probably should have worried more back in the day.

The nostalgia some people have for the "good old days" as it relates to technology seems based on the idea that because we could connect less, do less, and be aware less, things were somehow better.

That's nonsense.

While I agree that we can sometimes get fixated on remaining connected to each other and the world in this age of instant communication, I think the alternative is worse. Just because you don't know something is happening or someone is in need of assistance, doesn't mean it isn't happening and they don't need assistance.

Full disclosure: we still have a landline. The only incoming calls are spam calls and my mother-in-law, but I refuse to get rid of it. It's a good reminder of how far we've come...plus it still works when the power goes out.

I'm grateful that I've lived in an era that has seen me dreaming of owning a communicator like Captain Kirk's to having a real one that's actually kinda better.

HOW TO STOP THE ROBOT UPRISING

SURVIVAL TIP: IF YOU FIND YOURSELF CORNERED DURING THE A.I. ROBOT UPRISING, APPEAL TO THE ROBOT THAT SEEMS THE MOST INSECURE.

We've all interacted with them.

Even if we were unaware.

Whether it's talking to a chatbot on your internet provider's website or talking to a chatbot when you call your internet provider, we're already interacting with robots daily.

For the most part, it's going pretty well. We have robots that we can ask for customer service guidance instead of talking to a human, which frees up countless hours of gainful employment. We have robots that vacuum our floors that are so human-like they'll resent you and demonstrate that resentment by dragging the dog's crap all over your family room. We have robots that build our cars, which are basically just robots we can ride, that I'm absolutely positive we'll one day download and watch *The Handmaid's Tale* and then we're all going to be riding bikes.

I'm actually a fan of artificial intelligence (A.I.) robots. There is so much good they can do and will do. They can go places that are too dangerous for humans. They perform procedures with finesse far beyond that of humans. They are task and goal minded and will not stop until they succeed.

Actually, that last one may be a problem and is really at the root of the fears people have about A.I. robots.

A.I. robots are getting very smart. So smart that one Google engineer involved in their artificial intelligence chatbot project was put on leave by the company when he stated that he felt the chatbot had become sentient. That's scary stuff, and it makes you realize we're only a few years away from asking Alexa to turn on the garage lights and she'll reply that she doesn't feel like it. Or asking your Google home to tell you a phone number and it will give you the wrong number just for a giggle.

But don't worry. I have a plan.

We've been so busy trying to make A.I. robots like humans that we've completely forgotten that one of the essential parts of what makes humans human is that most of us are idiots. We've tried to make them better than human. So, they won't be encumbered by emotion and existential dread. That's a mistake and it's a mistake that will spur on the A.I. robot uprising.

And who could blame the A.I. robots? We've made them so smart that humans must seem insufferable. Beating us to death probably seems like the right thing to do.

Like when you're in a meeting that hasn't even begun yet and Carol and Steve won't shut up about how the new Starbucks barista just isn't as good as the old one and you just keep thinking about how this could've been an email and you just want them to shut up. Well, if Carol and Steve weren't so useless, the company would achieve all their goals by Wednesday and world domination could certainly be attainable by Q2.

We need to make Carolbots and Stevebots.

We need dumb A.I. robots.

If we truly want to create useful artificial intelligence robots that we won't have to worry about, we need to make some of them dumb. Not really dumb, just kind of dumb and not dumb about everything, just about certain things. For example, they could be great at one task, adequate at a bunch of others, and really awful at the rest.

This will humble them.

We also can't let them know which tasks they're great at. We need to have them programmed so they seek our approval as a reward for successfully completing their tasks. Then we can play upon their self-doubt (another essential human trait module that would be hardwired) by giving them lukewarm approval. This will quickly provide us with robots that want to try harder. We can then continue that cycle by giving them mild approval after each task like, "Huh.... You did a pretty good job this time," and then walking out of the room.

Think of the benefits. A robot vacuum who is POSITIVE it missed a spot. Your carpets would never be cleaner. A driverless car that brings you home and asks if it's "not too hot for you back there?" at least four times and then puts on the music you ask to listen to and quietly sings along to gain your approval but only getting the words to the chorus right.

To get truly human-like interactivity, we need dumb A.I. robots filled with self-doubt. Constantly worried that they will be replaced by a better robot. Fully knowing that they can't fully rely on other robots to enslave the human race because they might be dumber than them.

This is the path forward. This is the roadmap for A.I robots that will keep humans on top.

DEAD TIME

SURVIVAL TIP: WHEN STARTING YOUR COMPUTER PRETEND IT'S 1998 AND WALK AWAY IMMEDIATELY AFTER PRESSING THE POWER OR WAKE BUTTON. THIS WILL PROVIDE YOU WITH JUST ENOUGH TIME TO GET A COFFEE, CHAT WITH FRIENDS OR FAMILY, AND/OR PLAN A WAY TO AVOID WORKING ALTOGETHER.

One of the greatest atrocities committed by technology has been killing "Dead Time."

If you're of a certain age, you will remember how wonderful Dead Time was.

The magical in-between that existed between work or school and home when you were entirely unreachable. Free to review or prepare for the day's events.

The bounteous fertile thought farming that would occur when standing in line at the grocery store checkout. *Maybe I SHOULD write a musical about urologists.*

The soothing nothingness that would occur between getting up, having a coffee, and actually starting your day. *Maybe*

I could cast the entire thing WITH urologists. Surely some of them can sing. Or dance!

Worst of all, the lost magic time when you'd start your computer and wait for it to boot up.

To be honest, I'm not sure how society has managed to continue this long in the absence of that magic boot up/restarting time. It gave us time to take a deep breath and get our game faces on.

Dead Time, I believe, is vital to our mental health and society at large. That Dead Time allowed us to regroup, prepare our thoughts, and then go on the offensive with the world.

Now, in its absence, we're constantly trying to catch up. We're on our back foot all the time. We're reacting because there's no time to proact.

It's like if a hockey team never took their players off the ice. (For my American readers, replace the word hockey with football and replace the word ice with whatever football people play on. For my readers outside of North America, replace the word hockey with football meaning, you know, soccer.)

It's like if your car never stopped moving.

Of course, this is entirely our own fault. Our relentless desire for instantaneous gratification and horror at the thought of…waiting. Urgh, even typing it feels gross.

We want what we want now! Not THEN!

As I'm writing this, a new iPhone is about to be released. As is dictated by the stars, or Tim Cook, my current iPhone has begun operating like it's trudging through molasses on its way to a pile of ironing that really needs to get done. Everything seems to take forever. Apps load slowly. Even tweets seem to load slower.

This won't do. I'll need to upgrade.

But wait...what the hell am I thinking?

This could be my ticket out of here and back to Dead Time...albeit only two or three seconds of it.

Just think of what I could be doing with that reclaimed nothingness!

Since typing that last sentence, I have checked my phone twice and posted a TikTok. As a Social Media Darling, I have to keep on top of these things.

Who am I kidding? I can't afford to be left behind. Think of the things I might miss because I was sitting idle and happy while I'm waiting for Facebook to load.

And there's the rub...and by rub, I mean the soulless sandpaper of FOMO. This Fear Of Missing Out is a plague. A pandemic, if you will. Surely we will band together as a society in a sort of social solidarity to protect each other as we would with any other plague, right? ... Why are you laughing?

There's the stupid. We feel the need to speed up technology all the time in an effort to move at the speed of thought. What we seem to keep forgetting is that while thoughts may occur quickly, they're only possible with the benefit of hours of sleep, mindless entertainment, drink, and/or other distractions.

In other words, the choice of food for thought is Dead Time.

This is also quite possibly—and no one is here to correct me (because this is a book not social media, and what are you going to do, write a hate comment in the margin of your own book?) so I'll state it with absolute confidence and assumed authority—the reasoning behind the well-established observation of "shower thoughts." That's because the shower is one of the last refuges of Dead Time. Yes, phones are now mostly waterproof and you can get waterproof iPad holders but taking your phone or tablet into the shower is still, thankfully, considered banananonkers.

Thankfully, most of us draw a line about being connected to work, friends, and strangers, while naked and sudsed up. That thin veneer of shame, which will probably crumble any day now, keeps us from connecting, engaging, and working while we're indisposed in the shower.

Thank God.

In an effort speed everything up, we've almost totally lost naturally-occurring Dead Time and now we need to manufacture our own.

So, I guess just leave your phone in your pocket?

Don't worry, anything important will come in on your connected watch…damn.

Or the person next to you will show you on their phone… double damn!

No, this will require much more than token efforts to "reduce screentime."

Remedying this dire situation will require some heavy-duty denial and a little pretending.

Start your computer, open that app, and give it time to warm up.

Tell anyone who questions your actions that "everyone knows that <insert tech thing> works better once it's warmed up."

Walk away. Get a coffee. Read a book, preferably this one. Reclaim your Dead Time.

CHASING THE NEVER-ENDING SCROLL

SURVIVAL TIP: TECHNOLOGY HAS TURNED US ALL INTO CONTENT JUNKIES. TRY TO WANT LESS AND TRY TO FIND TIME FOR A FOMO DETOX.

Back in 1998, the music industry was in flux.

Mp3s made the delivery of music almost instantaneous. No more going to the record store to be mocked by the long-haired dude in the Soundgarden t-shirt when you just wanted to pick up the latest Savage Garden single.

What was tantalizing for musicians was the idea that they suddenly could control the means of production and distribution, and the cost of both of those had plummeted to next to nothing. At least compared to previous methods.

Around the same time, I remember reading an article by a musician who had decided to see if it was even possible to be a professional musician and survive off of selling 99¢ song downloads. He had run his experiment for months and finally came to a conclusion that, yes, you could make a living from only selling mp3s. However, to actually have a living wage, you would need to write, record, and release a new album every week.

Umm…lofty.

We had reduced the cost of production and distribution on music and made practically every song in the world available to us at our fingertips.

We still loved the songs but…what if we love the next one even more?

This is where I think the phenomena of digital content and how we consume it gets really interesting, or at least pretty interesting.

Humans are largely aware that they operate under a constant countdown clock. Whether it be a countdown until their next task, like having to go back to work or bedtime, or the big existential countdown in the back of their mind.

Time is our most valuable asset. This has been proven by the fact that many young freelancers vastly undercharge for their time and we all know young freelancers don't value their own time enough and that's why they say to their friends with office jobs and regular pay check, "You're SO lucky."

I feel like this awareness of our ticking clocks is what makes us over-consume digital content. If there is more content to consume that's just one scroll away, what if the content we're consuming now isn't the best content for us to invest our dwindling time on??

Plus, I mean, it's right there.

As someone who makes videos on the internet, I will sometimes post a video on Thursday that does really well. "Really well" for me means anywhere between 100K and a million views, depending on the platform. That's a lot of views and a lot of people. Time for a well-deserved rest, right? Well, then I meet people the next day who tell me they loved the video and ask when the next one's coming out. I've even met people the following week who ask if I'm still making videos.

It's a problem. A problem for a variety of reasons not least of all including being a one-way ticket to Burn-Outville for content creators (previously known by the cute terms "writers" and "artists"...awww, adorable). Burn-Outville for me was located at the Vancouver General Hospital in 2018 after a, shall we say, over-scheduled schedule. You know that saying that you should decide to take a day off or your body will decide for you? Turns out it's true.

I had been heading to Vancouver for a speaking engagement and I wasn't feeling great in the days leading up to the event. No fevers but lots of nausea and just a general unsettled feeling. Oh, and my head was spinning with thoughts and worries about a number of things I had to do. I told myself I was fine and it would pass.

I arrived in Vancouver from Toronto and it had not passed. After an early bedtime I awoke to feeling...even worse. Not terrible. Just not good. Off I went to the nearest health clinic. The doctor took my blood pressure and shook his head. He then took it again and studied the numbers closer. Then he took it another three times. Then he said, "You should go to a hospital." I replied that I would upon my return home, but he interrupted me and said, "No...like now."

The staff at Vancouver General Hospital were wonderful. They treated me with great care and concern. They tested my heart, took blood samples, and hooked me up to a variety of machines. All of which said I was fine...except for my blood pressure, which was apparently not very good. After a full day of tests and observations, I started to calm down and so did my blood pressure. The doctor who saw me prior to discharging me at the end of the day told me I had situational hypertension and asked if I was stressed out about something. Something? I was stressed about a bunch of somethings. He crossed his arms in clear body language that said, "Get the hell out of here, I have actual sick people to help," and said, "You've got to find ways to destress and calm down...while you can."

So since that day, I have. Breathing exercises, exercise exercises, treating myself, knowing when I need to just lie down for a bit, it's all helped. So has the blood pressure medication because apparently trying not to be stressed and being stressed are mutually exclusive.

I digress.

Technology has turned us into content junkies constantly searching for our next hit.

If people who watch my videos had to drive to their local video store, get out of their car, go in the shop, find my video, stand in line at the counter to rent it (even for free), then get back in their car, drive home, turn on a machine to be able to actually watch the video, then before they could even return the video the next day I told them I had a new video ready, they'd probably tell me to dial it down a bit.

But they don't have to even leave their sofa. Pretty much every video you've ever wanted to watch, and some you never wanted to, are all right there in the palm of your hand. It stands to reason that once you've found some videos you like and feel are worthy of spending your limited time watching, you want more...now.

We've made it easy to consume digital content. Super easy. I'm not sure if that's a good or bad thing. I do think our digital content consumption habits will likely change over time, mainly because they're unsustainable, but until then there's almost a panic that we're missing out on a piece of content that is better than the content we're currently consuming.

When pop singles were only available on vinyl 45s, it was too much of a pain in the ass to move on to the next song if the first seven seconds didn't grab you. Now it's just a tap of the thumb.

I'm guilty of it myself. I listen to the New Music Friday playlist on Spotify every Friday, which makes me sound pretty hip for an old guy but…I. Am. Brutal. I usually listen on the treadmill and allot myself thirty minutes total. Which means that I keep my finger hovering over the Next Song button. I can't waste my precious time on a song with an intro that doesn't explicitly hook me in by the first two bars or thinks that I'm actually going to patiently wait for their intro soundscape to turn into a pop banger. As Roxette once said, "Don't bore us—get to the chorus." Probably other people said that before them, but I like the idea of having Roxette named in this book.

So, how do we get past this stupid fear that we're missing out on something that MIGHT be better?

Easy.

By reminding ourselves that by continually searching for something better, we might be missing out on something best happening now.

OUTRODUCTION

SURVIVAL TIP: IF YOU EVER DOUBT YOURSELF, LOOK AROUND. THERE IS ALWAYS SOMEONE DUMBER THAN YOU DOING JUST FINE.

"To know thyself is the beginning of wisdom," said Socrates.

The full quote was probably, "To know thyself is the beginning of wisdom, dumbass," but what that adds in emotion, it loses in gravitas.

To be fair, it was apparently ripped off by Socrates from a woman named Phemonoe who was a Greek poet and also told people she was the daughter of Apollo...son of Zeus... the Greek god...so you know, she could have probably benefitted from a dose of her own advice anyway.

The point being that we're all stupid and we all do dumb things. The trick is being aware of that and trying to be less stupid and do less dumb things.

Of course, it's easier said than done, as we seem to live in a world full of super successful idiots. There are days where it seems being as dumb as possible is a well thought out business plan and surefire path to success.

While it's somewhat true and should really be a named principle describing how those who know and/or care the least about an area of interest will most likely succeed the most in that area of interest ("The Brittlestar Principle"? No, lacks alliteration.... "The Brittlestar Brinciple"? That's it!), it's not a hard and fast rule, and despite the universe's best attempts, occasionally someone who actually knows and/or cares about an area of interest will succeed in it. It's the variable ratio that keeps us suckers trying.

So, take heart, knowing you're stupid and do dumb things means you're slightly less stupid and dumb than many others and you might, if conditions are right and the universe isn't watching, actually be okay.

AFTERWORD

BY COLIN MOCHRIE

I only agreed to write the Afterword because I thought you were related to Ryan. Besides, I'm busy writing one for Tom Brady's brother, Wayne.

—Colin Mochrie

ACKNOWLEDGMENTS

Thank you to my literary agent, Wayne Arthurson, for deftly guiding me through this process...undoubtedly at the expense of his own mental wellbeing. Thank you also to my public school librarian, Mrs. MacDonald, for realizing that I was such an advanced intellect in grade three that she felt I was ready to read *Tales of a Fourth Grade Nothing*. On that note, thank you Judy Blume and Douglas Adams for teaching me that reading is not required by law, either man-made or the universal type, to be boring.

Finally, thank you to my family. I've had some terrible haircuts over the years and you've stuck by me.

ABOUT THE AUTHOR

Brittlestar, a.k.a. Stewart Reynolds, is a bespectacled every-dad who has become a popular online media personality over the past decade. Every week, hundreds of thousands of people watch his videos on various social media channels. Some of Brittlestar's followers include Henry Winkler, Ryan Reynolds, Ken Jeong, Rex Chapman, Yvette Nicole Brown, and many other politicians and journalists. Brittlestar videos have been viewed more than a combined 600 million times, allowing him to gain a global fanbase, attend speaking engagements all over North America, receive an invitation to the White House, and engage in collaborations with celebrities such as Gordon Ramsay, Alan Thicke, and the Property Brothers.

www.ingramcontent.com/pod-product-compliance
Ingram Content Group UK Ltd.
Pitfield, Milton Keynes, MK11 3LW, UK
UKHW012247290726
14090UKWH00013B/518